SPIRITUAL NAVIGATION

DISCERNING AND GROWING IN AUTHENTIC SPIRITUAL GIFTS AND EXPERIENCES

MARK HOFFMAN

Spiritual Navigation:
Discerning and Growing in Authentic Spiritual Gifts and
Experiences

Copyright 2020 by Mark Hoffman
All Rights Reserved

ISBN: 9781675487808

Unless otherwise indicated, scripture quotations are taken from the *New American Standard Bible®* *(NASB).* ©1960, 1962, 1963, 1968, 1971, 1972, 1973, 1975, 1995, by the Lockman Foundation. Used by permission.

For more content from Mark Hoffman, visit
www.foothillschurch.org/media/sermons or
www.foothillschurch.org/off-my-notes

Table of Contents

Chapter 1

The Current Climate

The daughter of a prominent televangelist stared into the studio's cameras with unwavering confidence. A hurricane was bearing down on the southern coast of the United States, promising catastrophic damage as the weather report scrolled past behind where she stood. She raised her voice and described how she knew that she could pray against this storm, and proceeded to do so with vigor, as two associates nodded along.

"We take an active role until this thing stops, dies down, and comes apart, and we know it," she said as she finished praying. "I have an expectation. Yep, it's coming apart. Harvey, did you know you're coming apart?" She flashed a joyful smile. "Harvey, did you know you're coming to nothing? Harvey, did you know you *obey* the Word of the Lord?"[1]

Soon after, Hurricane Harvey made landfall, causing 68 direct fatalities and causing an estimated \$125 billion in damage, making it the costliest tropical cyclone on record.[2]

In the aftermath, this daughter of a famed televangelist looked ridiculous, of course, and more fuel was added to the fire of those who would seek to defame the name of

---

[1] https://youtu.be/l2tNqGFQhOw
[2] https://en.wikipedia.org/wiki/Hurricane_Harvey

Christ and His people. This woman was quoting the Bible, praying, and full of confidence and what she called "faith," but the storm came anyway. She had said that God loves us, so this hurricane couldn't have its way, but it did.

This story raises questions for all of us who believe that God has the power to do miracles, heal, and that He has anointed us with His Holy Spirit. Are there limits to our spiritual authority in Christ, and if so, what are they? What about our power to heal? How can I live in the power of the Holy Spirit, and what does that mean? What are spiritual gifts, and how can they operate in my life? How do I become more discerning in my faith and practice?

The purpose of this book is to address these questions, and we will do so by looking to the Bible to find the answers. Jesus tells us in John 4:24,

God is spirit, and those who worship Him must worship in spirit and truth.

In order to worship God and walk with Him in a worthy manner, we must not only grow in becoming more spiritual, we must also grow into knowing the truth. The Bible is our source for growing in the truth.

Changing Times Bring Changing Questions

When I was first baptized in the Holy Spirit 43 years ago, much of the evangelical Church taught that the gifts of the Spirit were not for today, that they had mostly or entirely passed away at the end of the apostolic age. People's claims to be receiving these gifts were dismissed as a psychological delusion at best or a demonic delusion at worst. The subject of spiritual gifts was best left to the "Holy Rollers."[3] After we started our church, people were routinely warned to stay away from it because we were supposedly in error, since we practiced these charismatic expressions, or manifestations. We regularly had to defend ourselves against such charges.

However, as the influence of the Charismatic movement continued to grow among evangelicals, especially through the leadership of John Wimber and the Vineyard churches movement, the tide gradually began to shift. Today, the pendulum has swung so far that the greater problem now is a lack of discernment concerning spiritual gifts and spiritual manifestations. The current need is not so much to defend the reality of spiritual gifts but to teach people how to discern the genuine from the counterfeit.

America needs healthy churches and Christians that operate in the power of the Holy Spirit and all His wonderful gifts. Only then can the spiritual darkness that grips our nation be overcome and a wonderful harvest of new believers be brought in. This was Jesus' plan on the day He ascended to heaven, and it remains His plan today. Jesus desires you to be filled with the Holy Spirit and to be a part of His great works.

Having pastored the same charismatic church for almost 35 years, I have witnessed firsthand the power of the Holy Spirit to profoundly transform thousands of lives. In addition, we have had several seasons of powerful, special visitations that greatly built up our church and left our members with a greater love for Jesus and a deeper, more vital faith. But I have also witnessed churches that

---

[3] A pejorative title often given to members of Pentecostal denominations

claimed to have received a special visitation of the Holy Spirit left divided and diminished.

Some years ago, a church in our town brought in a so-called "revivalist" to spark revival at their church. The minister instituted meetings nearly every night of the week. There were some manifestations of the Spirit to be sure, and the emphasis was clearly on seeking them. They sold t-shirts and gave out bumper stickers to advertise the "revival" and did everything they could to promote it. There was great enthusiasm and excitement at first, but soon the crowds fell off and the church fell into divisions. Within several months the pastor was dismissed. The congregation continued to shrink, and today the church no longer exists. Its large facilities have been taken over by a charter school.

I have witnessed firsthand the good and the bad in the contemporary charismatic Church. I have not been a detached observer from afar. I have visited seven of the most celebrated "revivals" of the past 35 years. At some of them I have been invited behind the curtain and have talked with their leaders. I have also had the honor of meeting and becoming friends with a number of men who were national leaders of the Charismatic and Pentecostal movements. I have sat at their feet, dined in their homes, listened to their stories, and asked them questions.

Finding Balance

America needs revival. America needs churches that operate in the power of the Holy Spirit. But we must know how to discern the genuine from the false. If we are to be properly balanced, there are two opposite mistakes we must avoid.

The first error is to require that any reputed move of God be free from imperfections. It is also wrong to reject a group or movement because of the excesses of a few. There is no completely pure person, church, or movement. If God could only use a flawless person or movement, then He couldn't use anyone. Satan always attempts to use his wiles to sow a few tares in among the wheat. It is the nature of living in a fallen world, full of imperfect people, which requires that we practice discernment, if we are to stay balanced. We must know how to strain out the false in order to receive the true.

Do not quench the Spirit; do not despise prophetic utterances. But examine everything carefully; hold fast to that which is good. - *1 Thessalonians 5:19-21*

The second and opposite error is to refuse to discern or critique prophecies, spiritual manifestations, or teachings. It is a mistake to accept every manifestation or teaching. The Holy Spirit acts upon humans who can respond in inappropriate ways. Even anointed ministers can teach incorrect things. It honors, rather than offends, the Holy Spirit when we attempt to correct things in accordance with God's character and His inspired Word.

All of us should have the same goal of removing error and holding onto the good so that we might all benefit from it together. We must avoid the extremes of being skeptical on the one hand or gullible on the other. None of us should be so stiff-necked or proud that we can't examine our beliefs and practices together in the light of God's Word.

Practicing discernment doesn't mean that we divide up

into camps and criticize each other. Satan is our common enemy and the truth our common goal. We are to love one another since we are all brothers and sisters. All of us can benefit from listening to others in order to gain greater balance.

This book is written to help us learn the biblical principles which will allow us to effectively navigate the spiritual waters we encounter today. These waters are exciting but can also be deceptive.

The Outline of This Book

First, we will look at the challenges of living in a world that is both natural and spiritual. If we are being honest, we are far more comfortable and experienced in the natural than the spiritual. Being spiritual doesn't come naturally to us. We face certain difficulties as humans in responding rightly to God's Spirit which is both invisible and mysterious to us. Sometimes we can respond foolishly and get off track. In the chapter which follows, we will let the apostles Peter, James, and John be our guides to some common pitfalls.

In chapter 3 we will look at the purpose of God's anointing. God certainly has clear reasons for placing His Holy Spirit upon us. It is necessary that we understand those reasons.

In chapters 4 and 5 we will explore the important and fascinating subject of spiritual gifts.

Next, in chapter 6, we will consider how to grow in our ability to discern the genuine from the counterfeit in spiritual gifts and manifestations.

In chapter 7, we will turn our attention to the important role of the Church in helping us discover our gifts, guide us in their use, and give us opportunities to exercise them.

Then, in chapter 8, we will see how a proper understanding of the kingdom of God can help us answer burning questions we may have about our history in spiritual matters. Understanding God's kingdom is a great key in helping each of us make sense of our spiritual walk.

Following that, in chapter 9, we will explore the meaning of those special times of God-sent visitations and revivals. We will learn how to recognize them and how to receive the greatest benefit from them.

In the final chapter we will look ahead at God's incredible plans for the Church and world and learn how we can become His instruments in helping to bring these plans to fruition. God has a wonderful and challenging adventure ahead for each of us.

One last note before starting: This book is meant as a scriptural study of the subject of spiritual gifts and manifestations. While there are many scriptures quoted in the main body, for the sake of readability many others have been placed in the footnotes at the bottom of the page. The footnoted scriptures and notes are an essential part of the book. Please look them up as necessary where you have questions or need more clarity.

Chapter 2

Touched by the Glory

And [Jesus] was transfigured before them; and His face shone like the sun, and His garments became as white as light.   - Matthew 17:2

Some years ago at a high school summer camp, the presence of the Lord came during worship, and our plan for the night went right out the window. Kids were powerfully filled with the Spirit; many fell on their faces and others to their knees. Many wept and confessed sins as we ministered and prayed for them. It was hard to stand up straight under the weight of God's presence. Lives were changed that night by the incredible experience of the manifest presence of the Lord.

This was by no means a one-time occurrence. We have experienced many similar visitations over the years at church meetings, home groups, camps, and retreats. Sometimes these visitations have lasted for hours and other times God's presence has lingered with us for days—and on several occasions, even for weeks. Similarly, many people have reported to me a special time in their personal prayer time or worship when the presence of the Lord came down, touched them, and powerfully changed the atmosphere of the room.

These times are exciting and empowering, and often they can be life-changing. It is my sincere hope that we will continue to experience more of these times. As I have witnessed the different ways people have responded to the glory and power of God, it has raised important questions in my mind. Just how should we respond when God's glory and power come down? How should we view the extraordinary and unusual manifestations of His presence? What do these times mean? Can they ever become the norm for us? And finally, how should you think about some of the extreme ways you may have seen people respond in these settings?

A Mountaintop Experience

One particular story in the New Testament illustrates the divide between the natural and the supernatural. It demonstrates the sometimes misguided human response when God's glory and power come down to us, but it also shows us how God wants us to respond to His presence.

> *Six days later Jesus took with Him Peter and James and John his brother, and led them up on a high mountain by themselves. And He was transfigured before them; and His face shone like the sun, and His garments became as white as light. And behold, Moses and Elijah appeared to them, talking with Him. Peter said to Jesus, "Lord, it is good for us to be here; if You wish, I will make three tabernacles here, one for You, and one for Moses, and one for Elijah." While he was still speaking, a bright cloud overshadowed them, and behold, a voice out of the cloud said, "This is My beloved Son, with whom I am well-pleased; listen to Him!" When the disciples heard this, they fell face down to the ground and*

were terrified. And Jesus came to them and touched them and said, "Get up, and do not be afraid." And lifting up their eyes, they saw no one except Jesus Himself alone.
- Matthew 17:1-8

Wow. What a powerful scene of God's glory coming down along with spectacular manifestations! **Both Jesus and God the Father were present that day to help us understand His glory and to guide us into knowing how to respond.**

From the parallel account in Luke 9:28-36 we learn two additional facts: Jesus had gone to the mountain to pray, and just like when He went to the Garden of Gethsemane, Peter, James, and John fell asleep while Jesus was praying.

Now while Jesus is praying and communing with His Father, a change comes over Him. He is transformed into His future, glorious state. He shines as brilliant as the sun, so brilliant that it even radiates through His clothing. Two of the greatest figures from the Old Testament appear and begin speaking to Him: Moses the great lawgiver and Elijah, perhaps the greatest of the prophets.

By this time the three disciples are awake. Let's revisit the story at this point and watch what the disciples say and do.

Peter said to Jesus, "LORD, it is good for us to be here. If you wish, I will put up three shelters—one for you, one for Moses and one for Elijah."   - Matthew 17:4 NIV

Standing in the midst of this supernatural scene bathed in God's glory, Peter says something quite foolish. He suggests that He build them three shelters. Now, why would Moses and Elijah, in their glorified spiritual state, need a shelter built for them? They weren't like humans who might need a place to rest or shelter from the sun or cold. Certainly Jesus hadn't instructed him to build shelters.

Peter serves as a model of human nature. Even when the power of God is present, people are still people and can still think, do, and say foolish things. Even leaders like Peter. Here he is in the presence of Jesus, Moses, and Elijah, all who are in their glorified state, and his thoughts are on himself, his ideas, his abilities, and his usefulness.

The truth is that we can be where God is doing tremendous things and still be full of ourselves and our ideas, insecurities, and pride. This can make people do and say foolish and unhelpful things. This is why, even in the midst of God moving powerfully, we still need to practice discernment. You see, **experiencing God's glory and having supernatural experiences does not eliminate our flesh, sometimes it excites it.** Sometimes people can act in carnal and inappropriate ways when they are being touched by God.

I've seen people act in the wildest, most distracting manner, drawing much attention to themselves (and away from God), causing great confusion. Often it shuts down what God is trying to do in the lives of others. Some have left these so-called meetings confused, upset, and even fearful. This should not happen. The Bible tells us that God is not a God of confusion and disorder, therefore all things done in our meetings must be done in a fitting and orderly way.[4] Further, as Paul points out, when we don't do things in a fitting and orderly way, some will leave our meetings saying that we are merely crazy. However, when we do

---

[4] 1 Corinthians 14: 33, 40

things correctly, people will become convicted (convinced) by the Holy Spirit.[5]

This has certainly been our experience. We have very seldom seen people be resistant or even skeptical in the presence of the Holy Spirit's manifestations–if only fleshly outbursts are restrained and things are done in a way that honors God's holiness. Instead they are often profoundly touched and many repent and get saved. I am mystified why some people insist that the wilder and more chaotic a meeting, the more the Holy Spirit is in control.

Often people's highly emotional reactions are due to deep fears, insecurities, and wounds which require wise pastoral ministry rather than merely shouting, "More, Lord! Come on them even harder!" Oversight is necessary and pleasing to God when done correctly. If this wasn't so, then why did the apostle Paul write about how to maintain order during church services?[6]

The Problem of Ambition

This brings up another aspect of human nature that Peter's response shows us: The experience of Jesus' glory didn't eliminate Peter's ambition. After all, the tabernacle-building project was his idea, wasn't it? And to be implemented he would need help, and James and John were right there. I'm betting Peter assumed he would be in charge of this little construction project.

Personal ambition and insecurity can cause some people–even ministers who have the call of God on their lives and gifts evidenced in their ministry–to manipulate

---

[5] 1 Corinthians 14:23-32
[6] 1 Corinthians 14:26-40

others for their own ends, even if they don't fully realize they are doing it. The truth is that God must work through flawed individuals because these are the only kind of people available to Him. If God could only use perfect people, then He couldn't use any of us. That is why we must not just blindly follow any leader and why all of God's leaders must remain humble and open to correction.

Thankfully, in the midst of Peter's foolishness, the voice of God broke through:

While He was still speaking, a bright cloud overshadowed them, and behold, a voice out of the cloud said, "This is My beloved Son, with whom I am well-pleased; listen to Him!" When the disciples heard this, they fell face down to the ground and were terrified. - Matthew 17:5-6

Peter, James, and John had been full of themselves and slow to understand what was happening. Then suddenly God spoke and their flesh was silenced. They were humbled. God's Word brought reverence and the fear of the Lord.

Sometimes people think, "If only God would show up in spectacular manifestations of His presence, then everyone would become spiritual and live right." That's not how it worked for Peter, James, and John. It wasn't until God spoke that they stopped acting carnally. It is the same today. It is God's Word that brings God's order and spiritual maturity. An over-emphasis on our own ideas and subjective spiritual experiences can open the door to disorder and fleshly agendas. When God's Word is given its rightful place, God's order comes and His purposes are accomplished.

So what did God say? He said two key things:

1.) *"This is My beloved Son."*

Every true spiritual encounter must point to and magnify Jesus.[7] Jesus said of the Holy Spirit, *"He will glorify Me."*[8] It is the business of the Holy Spirit to glorify Jesus Christ—not the latest and greatest spiritual celebrity, angels, or the newest charismatic fad. Sometimes it even seems that Jesus is forgotten as people pursue these secondary things.[9]

2.) *"Listen to Him."*

God pointed the disciples beyond this powerful spiritual manifestation to the teaching of Jesus. Every true spiritual experience leaves us with a greater love, appreciation, and reverence for God's Word. It is not possible for a true encounter with the Holy Spirit to leave a person less committed to the teaching of the Bible. The Holy Spirit who inspired the scriptures will certainly draw people back to what He wrote, and He will not contradict it. Beware of people who resist or are annoyed when asked to explain the scriptural basis on which they are acting or ministering. After all, they are claiming to be animated by the same Holy Spirit who gave us the Bible.

This point can't be made too strongly. Any experience that leaves a person less committed to the Bible is not of God. It is perhaps the greatest spiritual deception to say, as

---

[7] 1 John 4:2-3
[8] John 16:14
[9] Fallen angels and deceiving spirits work to draw attention to themselves and away from Jesus.

some have said to me, "God speaks to me directly, so I don't feel the necessity to read the Bible much anymore." This attitude leads inevitably to the eventual replacement of God's Word with our own ideas and the changing norms of culture. One of the reasons God gives signs, wonders, miracles, and gifts of the Holy Spirit is to draw attention to His Word.[10] Ever since the beginning of the Church, God has used these things to validate the teaching of Jesus and the apostles:

> *For this reason we must pay much closer attention to what we have heard, so that we do not drift away from it....After it was at the first spoken through the Lord, it was confirmed to us by those who heard [i.e. the apostles], God also testifying with them, both by signs and wonders and by various miracles and by gifts of the Holy Spirit according to His own will.* - Hebrews 2:1, 3b-4

We must reject this far-too-common mistake of pitting the manifestations of the Spirit against the accurate teaching of the Bible, as if doing one diminishes the other. They are both the work of the same Spirit and must be held together. Be very cautious of meetings or groups where the Word of God is not given a central place.

Spiritual Authority

When God told the disciples to listen to Jesus, He was reminding them (and us) that they needed to submit to spiritual authorities. Something is wrong when spiritual experiences puff people up and make them think that they

---

[10] Hebrews 2:1-4, John 10:37-38

are beyond the leaders that God has given them. Jesus appointed pastors and elders to shepherd His Body, the Church.

The truth is that having spiritual encounters and experiences makes the ministry of pastors in our life more important, not less. We need a pastor's ministry to help us better understand our experience and know what to do in response. Pastors and elders are specifically gifted for this role of protecting and fostering those in their charge.

Obey your leaders and submit to them, for they keep watch over your souls as those who will give an account. Let them do this with joy and not with grief, for this would be unprofitable for you.   - Hebrews 13:17

It is troubling that in some movements today the biblical role of pastors and elders is downplayed. Many people are told that their experiences have catapulted them above their previous leaders and they no longer need listen to them. It has been heartbreaking to watch people fall into deception and even eventually fall away from the faith because they stopped respecting the position their pastors held in their lives. Properly called and recognized pastors do not hold you back from growth, but rather they are safeguards and aids in your spiritual growth.

Several years ago, a young leader at our church began hanging out with a group of older men that continually flattered him by telling him how very gifted he was. They told him that his abilities were not being appreciated at the church and that he had surpassed the spiritual under-standing of our church leaders. Although he was intrigued by their "prophecies," he had a strong, trusting relationship with me and had the good sense to come talk to me. The truth of the matter is that he was very appreciated, just young, and as the next several years passed he was given greater and greater responsibility. The men he had been hanging out with were self-deceived and filled with spiritual pride. They spoke critically of church leaders in an attempt to draw young people to themselves and to the brand of mystical spiritual deception they had fallen into.

Let's return to our story, picking it up in the next verse.

The Reality of Everyday Life

After God spoke and the disciples were silenced, Jesus touched them and said, "Get up, and do not be afraid" (Matthew 17:7). Notice what happens next:

And lifting up their eyes, they saw no one except Jesus Himself alone. - Matthew 17:8

This is everyday Christian life. The glory fades, and we are left to follow Jesus as our model.

The disciples wanted to build tents and stay in the glory experience, but Jesus leads them down the mountain to rejoin the other disciples and minister to a demon-possessed boy (Matthew 17:14-18). After the mountaintop experience, we are left with our daily walk with Jesus and our God-given responsibilities and callings.

Contrary to the teaching of some, mountaintop experiences are not meant to last forever or to be the normal Christian experience. Why? One reason is that God knows something about us: We can get used to anything. We become accustomed and conditioned to whatever we are constantly surrounded with until we grow numb to it. This is what psychologists call, "sensory adaptation." I'll give you an example:

When I was young, we lived above a freeway. My friends would come over and ask me, "How can you live here with all of that noise?" My brothers and I would always respond with, "What noise?" We had gotten so used to the constant buzzing of traffic that we didn't hear it anymore. Now, it's not just annoying things that we grow dull and accustomed to. We also grow accustomed to and take for granted beautiful and truly wonderful things like our daily food that God provides, the kindness of parents, the love of a spouse, or the stars in the heavens. We can even get to the point where the wonder of Christ's sacrifice on the cross no longer moves us.

Some might think that the manifestations of God are quite different than freeway noise or our daily bread, but remember the Israelites after they came out of Egypt. Every morning they woke up to a pillar of cloud in which God dwelt. Every night it became a pillar of fire lighting up the countryside. Every morning they woke up to a miracle as they were fed manna from heaven. Yet it didn't take long until they were no longer impressed. It was in the shadow of that pillar of cloud that they complained and wanted to return to Egypt. They became spiritually dull and complained constantly.

It's a terrible thing to become numb to the glory of God and to take it for granted. God's visitations and true manifestations must be rare enough that we continue to hunger for them and truly value them. That is why God, in His love, has determined that true visitations and revivals will never be so common that we grow dull toward them.

The demand for constant glory can lead to deception.

When the glory of a visitation begins to lift, as it must, some may try to recreate the same level of "manifestations" through emotional manipulation, hype, mysticism, and even demonic deception. The more people insist on living under constant glory, the more untethered their teachings become—along with more and more extreme behavior. They are ever in search of a higher high, naively chasing after more exotic and unbiblical manifestations.

What All This Means

Let's summarize some of the things we learned. It is wonderful to experience God's glory and presence. We should hunger, seek, and fervently pray for these things, and we should never be satisfied with lives or meetings that are devoid of His glory and presence.

At the same time, we must realize that times of divine visitation and expressions of divine manifestations are determined by God alone. The Bible tells us that the Holy Spirit distributes gifts and manifestations "just as He wills"—not as we will.[11] It is significant that the glory fell on the mountain of transfiguration while the disciples slept. We should be wary of people who claim to be able to control times of visitation or spiritual manifestations.

Every true spiritual experience or manifestation should focus us more on Jesus. They should also make us more humble and bring about a greater love and respect for our churches and leaders. This will make us more fruitful in the ministries He has appointed us to and will lead to greater evangelism, unity, and the advance of Christ's kingdom.[12]

---

[11] 1 Corinthians 12:11

[12] Jesus led the disciples down from the mountain to minister to a demonized child. See Matthew 17:17 and following.

The Holy Spirit has a clear purpose in His working among us. In the next chapter we will look at what the Bible says about the anointing of the Holy Spirit.

Chapter 3

The Anointing
of the Holy Spirit

*But you will receive power when the Holy Spirit has come
upon you; and you shall be My witnesses both in Jerusalem,
and in all Judea and Samaria, and even to the remotest part
of the Earth.   - Acts 1:8*

What made Jesus so unique?

Well, obviously He is God and we aren't. He was born
without sin and therefore had no sin nature. He was,
however, still fully man as well, subject to all the same
temptations and struggles as you and me.[13]

Jesus was not born with natural advantages. He was
not born in a palace but a stable. He was not born to
wealth. His father died while he was still young. Nor was
He especially handsome. He was not a physically imposing
figure. The closest thing we have to a physical description
of Jesus comes from the prophet Isaiah:

*He had no beauty or majesty to attract us to Him, nothing
in His appearance that we should desire Him.*
- Isaiah 53:2, NIV

---

[13] Hebrews 4:15

It may amaze you to realize that when the Creator of the entire universe sent His Son to earth, He didn't make Him a natural standout. He was apparently quite average.

I regularly talk to people who are angry or dejected at the way that God made them or the circumstances of life they were born into. They think that God shorted them something that they need to be happy or successful. But consider this: God did not think it necessary to give His Son natural advantages. None of those things were necessary to Jesus' success, and they are not to ours either.

Jesus' advantage was a supernatural one, one that is available to us as well. This advantage is revealed in the name by which we know Him: Jesus Christ, or more properly, Jesus the Christ. The title "Christ" means "Anointed One." It is the Greek translation of the Hebrew word "Messiah." From the time of the Old Testament prophets, the Jews had been waiting for the Messiah, one who would be uniquely anointed by the Holy Spirit.

To anoint means to pour or rub oil onto someone or something. Oil was greatly valued in the ancient world because of its healing, cleansing, and restoring properties. Oil became a symbol of the Holy Spirit because He also heals, cleanses, and renews.

We have an extensive record of Jesus' life, miracles, healings, and teachings from the time He was 30 years old until His death, burial, and resurrection. But the Bible does not record any miracles, healings, or ministry to great crowds before that. It states clearly that His ministry began at age 30.[14] What changed? At age 30, Jesus was baptized and the Holy Spirit descended upon Him in the form of a

---

[14] Luke 3:23

dove.[15] This was when Jesus became anointed with the Holy Spirit and His miraculous ministry could begin.

After Jesus' baptism He was led into the wilderness to fast, pray, and overcome Satan's temptations. Then He returned to His hometown to announce the beginning of His public ministry.

> *And Jesus returned to Galilee* **in the power of the Spirit**. *...And He came to Nazareth, where He had been brought up; and as was His custom, He entered the synagogue on the Sabbath, and stood up to read. And the book of the prophet Isaiah was handed to Him. And He opened the book and found the place where it was written, "The Spirit of the Lord is upon Me, because* **He anointed Me** *to preach the gospel to the poor. He has sent Me to proclaim release to the captives, and recovery of sight to the blind, to set free those who are oppressed, to proclaim the favorable year of the Lord." ...And He began to say to them, "Today this Scripture has been fulfilled in your hearing."* - Luke 4:14, 17-19, 21, emphasis added

Look at two key phrases in the passage above: *"in the power of the Spirit"* and *"He anointed Me."*

Jesus' life and ministry were radically changed after the anointing He received at the time of His baptism. The Bible teaches us that though Jesus was fully God in nature, He emptied Himself of His divine privileges, like being all-powerful and all-knowing, and took on the limitations of a human being.[16] That means that He did nothing of His own initiative, but He was instead

---

15 Luke 3:21-22
16 Philippians 2:6-8

entirely dependent upon the Father, providing us with a picture of how we ought to be dependent on God.[17]

We should also be anointed by the Holy Spirit. We are called Christians, which literally means "little Christs" or "little anointed ones."

Now, Jesus was unique in the depth and breadth of the anointing. The Bible tells us that He was given the anointing of the Holy Spirit in complete fullness, or without measure.[18] We, however, receive just a measure of this same anointing of grace.[19] Nevertheless, His life is in many ways an example of how we can operate in the Holy Spirit's power, gifting, and wisdom.

Just as Jesus' anointing set Him apart and empowered Him to do great works of God, we also are supposed to be set apart by the anointing of the Holy Spirit. The anointing is the difference between who you are in your own strength and who you are in His. For some of you, it could be the difference between the life you are living now and the life you could be living. All of us can seek a deeper expression of the Holy Spirit in our lives.

In order to fully understand this, we have to look deeper into the concept of anointing. In ancient Israel, kings, prophets, and priests were anointed. Oil represents the Holy Spirit, and the idea was that in the symbolic act of pouring oil on the head of, for instance, a new king, he would receive the authority, ability, and wisdom to rule and shepherd God's people. The anointing represents God's enablement coming on a person.

I want us to look at the three different types of

---

17 John 5:19,30
18 John 3:34-35
19 Ephesians 4:7

anointing that we find in the Old Testament. These are the Leper's Anointing, the Priest's Anointing, and the King's Anointing. These reveal important truths about how, through the Holy Spirit, we can be set apart for God and enabled to live out His purpose for us.

Anointing #1: The Leper's Anointing

Then the Lord spoke to Moses, saying, "This shall be the law of the leper in the day of his cleansing."
- Leviticus 14:1

You can't read the Bible for very long and miss the many references to lepers and leprosy. These include Miriam's temporary judgement of leprosy, Naaman's cleansing from leprosy, King Azariah struck with leprosy, the ten lepers healed by Jesus, etc. In fact, lepers and leprosy are referenced 68 times—far more than any other disease. This is because of its symbolic nature. **Leprosy became a symbol for sin because it shares so many of its characteristics.** This accounts for the many regulations concerning it in the Law of Moses. Leprosy is used as an object lesson to teach God's people what sin looks like and what it does to people.

First, both leprosy and sin *desensitize* us. Leprosy attacks the nerves so that you lose your sense of feeling. One of the reasons that leprosy disfigures people is that they no longer feel pain. As a result, they suffer from burns, infected cuts, preventable injuries, and they often put off getting needed medical attention. Sin is the same. It desensitizes our conscience. It dulls us to the conviction of the Holy Spirit and His leading, as well as the feelings of others.

Also, sin and leprosy are both **progressive**. Leprosy begins as just a small patch but if left untreated, it continues to grow and spread across your body, bringing increasing disfigurement. Sin does the same thing. If you willingly accept even some small sin into your life, you will find that you can't contain it. That compromise with sin will begin to spread into other areas of your life bringing increasing damage.

Both sin and leprosy **separate** people. They break up families and communities. People with leprosy had to be separated from their families and community and live outside the city walls and far from villages. Think of how many marriages, families, and communities have been destroyed by sin.

Finally, both **lead to death**.

However, God can cure sin, and in Leviticus 14 we see the ceremony prescribed to declare a person who was once leprous to now be clean:

First, the former leper received a visit from the priest outside of camp. If he determined that the leprosy had gone, he would order two birds to be brought out. The first bird was sacrificial; it was killed in an earthenware jar over running water. The second bird was dipped in the blood of the first, and then the one who is to be cleansed from leprosy was sprinkled seven times with the blood. Then, the bird was released to go free in an open field.

The symbolism is important: The bird in an earthenware jar represents Jesus, who came down in a human body (like the jar created from clay) and was sacrificed for our sin. It was sacrificed over running water to foreshadow the fact that the benefits of this sacrifice would come to us through the waters of baptism. Even in the Old Testament, long before Jesus was born, this ceremony pictured God's future plan for our salvation and forgiveness.

The wonderful truth is that we are forgiven and set free by the blood of Jesus, just as the second bird was set after free being dipped in the blood of the one that was killed.

As incredible as this is, it is only the first part of the ritual. Now, if it was only a question of forgiveness, the ceremony would be over. But sin also has the power to hold us captive, to take away our freedom and to distort our perception of the world. **Anger, bitterness, addictions, and other vices not only need to be forgiven, but their power over us needs to be broken.** Sins become compulsions that cause us to destroy our lives, our families, our potential, and our future happiness.

After the leper was sprinkled with the first bird's blood and the second bird was released, the priest would take oil and sprinkle it before the Lord and then smear it on the leper's right earlobe, his right thumb, the big toe of his right foot, and then the rest would be poured out on his head.[20] The oil which symbolizes the anointing of the Holy Spirit was:

> • First applied to the ear, which represents the five senses of the body and their lusts, to show that their power can be broken in Christ.
>
> • Next the thumb and hand which represent a person's actions, sinful habits, and addictions, whose power is broken in Christ.

---

[20] To find more details from the ceremony, read Leviticus 14:1-20.

• Then the toe and foot, representing a person's walk or manner of life. Destructive habits and lifestyles can be overcome by the power of Jesus' blood and replaced with a new lifestyle in Christ.

• Finally, the rest of the oil was poured out on the head of the leper to show that the Holy Spirit can redeem even our thoughts, conquering the lies that we've believed, sinful thought patterns, fears, compulsive thinking, and anything else not of God's truth and goodness. The anointing of the Holy Spirit allows us to have a renewed mind.

And do not be conformed to this world, but be transformed by the renewing of your mind.   - Romans 12:2 [21]

The anointing of the Holy Spirit shatters the power of sin over us, with its addictions, lusts, and destruction. It empowers us to live differently, to live a fruitful life that is pleasing to God.

I've seen this power at work in hundreds, even thousands of lives. I have known its power in my own life. I was in bondage to alcoholism, struggling with periods of deep depression. But when I received Christ's forgiveness, I received the Leper's Anointing as well. One touch from God set me free from sin's destructive power. The Holy Spirit empowered me to walk differently, the chains of my bondage broken. Often, this deliverance is a process, but it is always accomplished by the power of the Holy Spirit.

Many are held by sin's power, unable to break free no matter how hard they try. It may be alcoholism, drug addiction, pornography, unforgiveness, anger, despair—the list could go on. We may label it as a sickness or disorder. We might blame others and spend a lifetime trying to manage our problem. But when we agree with God and call it sin, we can be set free from its power. After all, Jesus didn't die for "oppositional defiance disorder," He died for the sin of anger and rebellion. Until you call it what it is, you cannot receive the Leper's Anointing. But when you confess it as sin and ask for forgiveness and cleansing, you can be free.

> *If we say that we have no sin, we are deceiving ourselves and the truth is not in us. If we confess our sins, He is faithful and righteous to forgive us our sins and to cleanse us from all unrighteousness. - 1 John 1:8-9*

Anointing #2: The Priest's Anointing

> *The holy garments of Aaron shall be for his sons after him, that in them they may be anointed and ordained.*
> *- Exodus 29:29*

The Priests' Anointing found in Exodus 29 is a testament to the holiness of God. Only the priests were allowed to draw near to God on behalf of the people and themselves. Everyone who was to become a priest had to be anointed before they could minister at the Temple.

In order to ordain a priest, God set out a ceremony for the Israelites to follow.[22]

The priests-to-be would lay their hands upon a bull that would then be sacrificed. Next, a ram was brought out and

---

[21] See also Ephesians 4:22-23
[22] For greater detail of the Priest's Anointing ceremony, read Exodus 29.

sacrificed in a similar manner. The reason the priests would lay their hands on the sacrificial animals was to symbolize the transference of their sins to the animal. Some of the blood would be sprinkled on the priests to foreshadow the fact that it is because of the blood of Christ that we are able to approach our holy God and minister as priests.[23]

The ceremony also involved the priest being washed with water, symbolizing the removal of sin and uncleanness such as happens to us through the washing of baptism and the Word.[24] Next there was an exchange of clothing. Their clothes were removed and replaced with beautiful, white, priestly clothes just as we are clothed with the righteousness of Christ.

Finally, the anointing oil would be poured on the head of the priests and on their priestly garments. This is because you can take a person and wash him on the outside and put him in new clothes and still have the same person inside. It is the Holy Spirit that changes the heart.

This anointing signifies an inward change. The Priest's Anointing takes us beyond the Leper's Anointing. It's one thing to be a leper and receive forgiveness and be delivered from the power of sin's hold, it's quite another to be a priest—and God calls us to be priests.[25]

A priest is a bridge. He speaks to people on behalf of God and prays to God on behalf of people. In order to do this, a priest must have a deep love for God and compassion for people, but this is contrary to human nature.[26] The heart is naturally selfish, alienated from God, and critical or

---

[23] Hebrews 4:16
[24] 1 Corinthians 6:11; Ephesians 5:26
[25] 1 Peter 2:9
[26] Romans 8:7-8

indifferent toward people, so in order to be a priest there has to be an inward change by the power of the Holy Spirit.

Moreover, I will give you a new heart and put a new spirit within you; and I will remove the heart of stone from your flesh and give you a heart of flesh. I will put My Spirit within you and cause you to walk in My statutes, and you will be careful to observe My ordinances. - Ezekiel 36:26-27

The Priest's Anointing looked forward to a time when God would give His people an inward change brought about by the Holy Spirit. He promised to give us a new heart, meaning that we would be responsive to God and His ways. He would replace the desire to sin with an inflamed love for God. This would allow us to do His work of representing Him on the earth and of interceding for those who need Him.

Before the Lord changed my heart, I had no desire for the Bible. I didn't want to hear songs of praise, and I didn't see much point in prayer. I avoided church at all costs. But once God anointed me, I had new desires! I didn't want to get drunk anymore; I wanted to share the love of Jesus. I loved hearing God's Word. I was excited to pray. I loved His Church, whereas I didn't before. I now had love in my heart for God and for the people that He created. My inward thoughts and responses were transformed.

The fruit of the Spirit is love, joy, peace, patience, kindness, goodness, faithfulness, gentleness, self-control.
- Galatians 5:22-23

We cannot accomplish God's role for us in this world

or draw near to Him without a new heart. We need to look each day to the Priest's Anointing for the power to love God, have compassion on our fellow man, and live a life of joy and faithfulness.

Anointing #3: The King's Anointing

Then Samuel took the horn of oil and anointed him in the midst of his brothers; and the Spirit of the Lord came mightily upon David from that day forward.
- 1 Samuel 16:13

The King's Anointing is shown in 1 Samuel 16, and it's simple. The new king-to-be had oil poured over his head. Every king starting with Saul[27] was to be anointed in this way. We need to ask ourselves, "Why did David and all of the other kings need an anointing from the Holy Spirit?"

As the leader of his nation, the ancient king was a warrior who led his troops in battle. He also acted as a judge and legislator, making laws and enforcing them. In short, he was a decision-maker. A king needed strength and courage to wage victorious war, and he also needed wisdom to lead God's people.

You and I have to war in this world. 1 John 5:19 tells us:

We know that we are of God, and the whole world lies in the power of the evil one.

Yet Ephesians 6:12 reminds us:

Our struggle is not against flesh and blood, but against the

---

[27] 1 Samuel 10

rulers, against the powers, against the world forces of this darkness, against the spiritual forces of wickedness in the heavenly places.

Every day we are involved in a spiritual battle. God has given us this anointing to prevail.

This King's Anointing is what we commonly refer to as "baptism in the Holy Spirit." John the Baptist referred to this:

As for me, I baptize you with water for repentance, but He who is coming after me is mightier than I, and I am not fit to remove His sandals; He will baptize you with the Holy Spirit and fire.   - Matthew 3:11

1 Corinthians 12:8-10 talks about nine gifts of the Holy Spirit for powerful ministry (more on these in the next chapter). These are manifestations of the King's Anointing. Some Christians know about water baptism but are not acquainted with the baptism in the Holy Spirit. This is the anointing by which we cast out demons. It's by the King's Anointing that we pray for the sick. When we witness to others, we ought to do it in the King's Anointing. When a pastor preaches, he must lean on the King's Anointing, knowing that his own cleverness is not sufficient to change people's hearts. We all need the power of the Holy Spirit.

Consider this: Jesus' apostles received the first two anointings (Leper's and Priest's) when Jesus breathed on them and said, "Receive the Holy Spirit."[28] Even still, Jesus told them not to begin their ministry until they received the King's Anointing at Pentecost. We can't be effective for

---

[28] John 20:22

Christ without this anointing.

It was only through the guidance and empowering of the Holy Spirit that these few outcast men could fulfill Jesus' charge to them: To spread this illegal, unpopular, oppressed faith to the entire world. The Holy Spirit was intimately involved, and He is still working today. Without the Holy Spirit's anointing, they could not succeed. It is the same for you and me.

The Purpose of the Power

What is the reason for this baptism of power? As with any spiritual experience, we need to examine its purpose because failure to understand this leads to misuse. Today, there is much confusion regarding the baptism of the Holy Spirit, and it's led to some troubling extremes.

Our God is a God of purpose. He always acts with purpose. So we have to ask, "What was the reason that Jesus sent us the baptism of the Holy Spirit?" He explains in the first chapter of Acts:

> *But you will receive power when the Holy Spirit has come upon you; and you shall be My witnesses both in Jerusalem, and in all Judea and Samaria, and even to the remotest part of the earth. - Acts 1:8*

Jesus' main purpose in sending the Holy Spirit was to empower His Church to reach the lost. On the day of Pentecost, when the Holy Spirit was poured out, 3,000 souls were saved. The truest measure of the Holy Spirit's activity is not exotic, controversial manifestations but rather people getting saved, baptized, and delivered. We can be certain of this because it is what Jesus sent Him to do.

The Holy Spirit's work has two dimensions: The inner work, which accomplishes regeneration and sanctification inside of the believer, and the outer work of empowering the believer to destroy the works of the devil[29] and to set people free. Jesus' primary purpose in pouring the Holy Spirit upon the Church is for evangelism. Recall the prophecy that Jesus quoted in the synagogue on the day He began His ministry:

> *The Spirit of the Lord is upon Me, because He anointed me to preach the gospel to the poor. He has sent Me to proclaim release to the captives, and recovery of sight to the blind, to set free those who are oppressed, to proclaim the favorable year of the Lord.* - *Luke 4:18-19*

Although we receive a lasting anointing to be free from sin's power and receive a new heart as priests and have kingly power, we can also receive fresh anointing of these powerful provisions when we need it.[30] Many times while ministering, or in the face of some challenge, I have felt the power of the Holy Spirit come on me afresh.

Putting It Together

Jesus came that we might have all three anointings:

The Leper's Anointing: Forgiveness, Salvation, and Deliverance

The Priest's Anointing: Sanctification and the Fruit of the Spirit

The King's Anointing: Power and Gifts of the Spirit

---

[29] 1 John 3:8
[30] Judges 6:34; 14:19; Acts 4:31

To walk in just one of these anointings is to stop short of what the Lord desires for us. Two is not enough either. We have to operate in all three anointings, all of which are by the same Spirit of God who is calling the lost to repentance and His people to holiness.

In the next two chapters we will look at spiritual gifts, which are an important element of the King's Anointing.

Chapter 4

Spiritual Gifts Part I:
The Manifestation Gifts

Now concerning spiritual gifts, brethren, I do not want you to be unaware. - 1 Corinthians 12:1

When bad things happen, many Christians ask, "Why?"
"Why did this happen to me?"
"Why does God allow this evil?"
"Why is this person suffering?"

People agonize over such questions, but they are the wrong things to ask. Instead of "Why?" we ought to ask "How?" and "What?" When something bad happens, we should ask, "*How* can I glorify Christ in this situation?" and "*What* grace has God set aside for me to overcome in this situation?"

The Bible assures us that God is so great that He can cause all things to work together to bring about good.[31] He is greater than any difficulty. God can cause us to be triumphant under any circumstance.

Being assured of this, we need to stop being intimidated and defeated by problems that arise in life. We ought to instead take courage in God's promises to give us the

---

[31] Romans 8:28

needed grace. He has promised that His grace is sufficient for us[32] and that He will always lead us in triumph.[33] Our focus needs to be on how we can lay hold of God's grace and assistance in every situation.

By His supernatural empowering, God enables us to do what we otherwise could not do. He lifts us above our human limitations and brings us into His possibilities. One form of this grace is spiritual gifts. In 1 Corinthians 12-14, Paul provides us with an excellent study of this supernatural empowering. In the first two verses of chapter 12, he introduces us to both the importance and the risks of spiritual gifts:

> *Now concerning spiritual gifts, brethren, I do not want you to be unaware. You know that when you were pagans, you were led astray to the mute idols, however you were led.*
> *- 1 Corinthians 12:1-2*

Paul begins by stating that he doesn't want us to be misinformed or ignorant regarding spiritual gifts.[34] God's enabling power is a vital part of His plan and provision for us. We fail to honor Him when we remain ignorant of the ways in which He works through His people.

Unfortunately, this is all too common. Many Christians and even many churches seem to ignore spiritual gifts, but the truth is the Christian life can't be lived by human strength alone. The cause of Christ cannot be accomplished by mere human talent and training.

---

[32] 2 Corinthians 12:9

[33] 2 Corinthians 2:14

[34] The word in the original Greek, "pneumatikon," can be more broadly translated as "spiritual matters" or "things of the spirit."

We need the gifts that the Holy Spirit has for us, but we receive an important warning in verse 2. Spiritual gifts and experiences have counterfeits.

The believers in Corinth had been pagans before finding Jesus. They had experienced ecstatic trances, visions, physical shaking, and false prophecies, and these deceptive spiritual experiences led them astray. Therefore, they needed to be alert to the possibility of spiritual deception. After all, the Holy Spirit is not the only spirit we can encounter in the spiritual realm, and Satan is a master counterfeiter.[35]

It's an undeniable principle: everything that is valuable will be counterfeited. Think about it. We have counterfeit money because money is valuable. Famous paintings sell for a high price, so we have to watch out for forgeries. Likewise, spiritual gifts are to be greatly desired, so we must be prepared for counterfeits that are not from God. It is important to remember that there would not be any counterfeits if there was not something real for them to imitate.

Today we find an increased hunger for spiritual experiences, spiritual gifts, and prophecies. With this increased openness we can expect an increase in spiritual counterfeits and deceptions. This is how Satan works.

Many Christians seem to gravitate to one extreme or the other. Either they become overly cynical and suspicious because of the counterfeits, or they race ahead and un-critically accept everything that is seemingly supernatural. So what is the proper response?

---

[35] 2 Corinthians 11:14

Separating the True from the False

Consider this, no one burns their money because they realize there is counterfeit money in circulation. Art dealers don't stop buying art just because some paintings are forgeries. We shouldn't turn our backs on spiritual gifts either—instead we need to be able to tell the imitations from the real thing.

It is often said that the best way to recognize the counterfeit is to become very familiar with the genuine. For instance, bank tellers are taught to recognize counterfeit money by first becoming very familiar with the feel of genuine money. By learning what genuine money feels like they can feel the difference in the counterfeit. **Likewise, we grow best in our ability to recognize what is false by understanding and using what is true. Instead of fearing the counterfeits we should pursue the genuine.** Jesus said that when we come to recognize His voice as our Good Shepherd, we will not be deceived to follow other voices.[36]

The Corinthians needed to be able to tell the genuine gifts from the counterfeits. Their city was filled with mediums, soothsayers, and pagan priests—and some of them were now converts to Christ. The believers at Corinth wanted to know how to tell the genuine.

In verse 3 of our passage, Paul gives us and them a simple test: Every true activity of the Holy Spirit will elevate the lordship of Jesus Christ, and every activity of false, lying spirits will seek to diminish the lordship of Jesus Christ. Any spirit, gift, or minister that does not lift up

---

[36] John 10:3-5, 27

Jesus Christ as He has defined Himself in the New Testament is not authentic.

> *Therefore I make known to you that no one speaking by the Spirit of God says, "Jesus is accursed"; and no one can say, "Jesus is Lord," except by the Holy Spirit.*
> *- 1 Corinthians 12:3* [37]

Spiritual Gifts Bring Unity

The church at Corinth was full of spiritual pride and divisions, which even a quick read of 1 Corinthians reveals.[38] It's not surprising that they also had divisions over spiritual gifts. They fought over which gifts were most important, how they ought to be used in public meetings, and what their purpose was. (Chapters 12-14 were written to address these problems.) Paul shows us that spiritual gifts are meant to bring unity, not to increase divisions. After all, spiritual gifts flow out of the unity of the Godhead.

> *Now there are varieties of gifts, but the same Spirit. And there are varieties of ministries, and the same Lord. There are varieties of effects, but the same God who works all things in all persons.   - 1 Corinthians 12:4-6*

---

[37] There are other tests that the Bible gives us as well, such as the witness of the Old Testament scriptures (Isaiah 8:19-21), the New Testament writings of the apostles (1 John 4:6), and the fruit of the manifestation or minister (Matthew 7:15-17). We will explore this issue in more detail later.

[38] They divided over such things as which leaders were most important (chapters 3-4), marriage, celibacy, and divorce (chapter 7), restrictions on food (chapters 8-11), public worship (chapters 11 and 14), the Lord's Supper (chapter 11), and the nature of our resurrection (chapter 15).

Notice that gifts are associated with the Holy Spirit, ministries with Jesus, and the effects or end results with God the Father. Therefore, a diversity of gifts, ministries, and effects should create unity since one triune God is behind them all. Each member of the Trinity plays a role.

The Holy Spirit gives spiritual gifts. Think of what a gift is—something unearned. You don't have to qualify before I give you a gift. It isn't a payment or a reward. I give it to you as a token of my favor. The same is true of spiritual gifts. The Holy Spirit doesn't give them to you because you are good but because God is. The greatest gift God gives us is salvation. If God gives that gift freely, how much more will He give every other gift?

Therefore, you don't have to attain to a certain level of maturity to receive a spiritual gift. Anyone who has accepted Jesus as Lord and Savior can receive them through the Holy Spirit. He gives these gifts freely, not like badges or trophies. This is why the Holy Spirit will do supernatural things even through very imperfect and immature Christians.

Jesus appoints people to ministries. Ministries, on the other hand, are different from gifts. Ministries are ongoing platforms or positions, usually recognized by the church, so we have a wider opportunity to use our gifted-ness. Think of something like leading a Sunday school class or a home fellowship, getting invitations to minister at other churches, or some other form of recognized leadership. These are appointed by our Lord Jesus, who distributes them based upon Christian maturity and are given to those who demonstrate godly and proven character.[39]

---

[39] 1 Timothy 3:1-13, 5:9-10; Titus 1:6-9

Continuing in a given ministry depends upon continued faithfulness. Unfaithfulness and immorality will lead to being removed from the appointed position.[40] Though unfaithfulness will lead to a loss of ministry position, a person may still continue to function in the area of spiritual giftedness—at least for a time. This is why apparent spiritual giftedness is not, by itself, a reliable indicator of whether someone is trustworthy.

God the Father determines results. The Bible teaches that the outcome and effect of these gifts and ministries is from God the Father, Who is the source of all. God works in all these things for the benefit of His people, and His purposes are accomplished by them.

Just as spiritual gifts and ministries flow out of the unity of the Trinity, so they are to bring about the unity in the Body of Christ. Paul clearly emphasizes and illustrates this truth later in this same chapter (1 Corinthians 12: 12-27). The divisions in today's Church due to the misunderstanding and misuse of spiritual gifts is truly heartbreaking. This is certainly an area where humility and a willingness for correction are needed.

The Purpose of the Gifts

God's motive in giving these gifts and ministries is given in the next verse:

> *But to* **each one** *is given the* **manifestation** *of the Spirit for the* **common good***.*
> *- 1 Corinthians 12:7, emphasis added*

---

[40] See Revelation 2:5, where the lampstand refers to the authority to represent Christ's witness.

There are three key phrases that we need to focus on in the above scripture:

- *"Each one"*
- *"Common good"*
- *"Manifestation"*

Since we don't have to qualify for or deserve spiritual gifts, "each one" can be given one. Spiritual gifts are not just for pastors, traveling ministers, or spiritual superstars. God wants to give spiritual gifts to all of His children. He wants to use you. The real issue is not your worthiness but your availability.

Note also that these gifts are given for the *"common good"* or the good of all. They are given for the benefit of the Church, not for the glory or financial benefit of the one through whom the gift comes. Spiritual gifts are generally given through us to benefit another who needs God's compassion and help, or for the benefit of the larger group. For instance, as a general rule, people don't lay hands on themselves and receive a healing. The healing almost always comes through another person.[41] This is in the purpose of God to build unity and interdependency among the members of the Body.[42] Spiritual gifts are a call to serve others, not ourselves.

The word translated *"good"* here is the Greek word "symphero," which can also translated as "advantage," as it is two times in the New Testament.[43] Spiritual gifts are

---

[41] The wording of James 5:16 is interesting to note here.

[42] 1 Corinthians 12:12-27

[43] As in John 16:7 when Jesus tells the disciples it is to their advantage that He leaves them and goes to heaven so that He can send them the Holy Spirit. See also 2 Corinthians 8:10.

given so that we may gain an advantage over our enemy. When we ignore or fail to use them, we give up this advantage and suffer needless defeats. If we are to see greater victories in the Church, we must understand and rightly use spiritual gifts.

Finally, our third word "manifestation" is key to understanding these gifts.

The Manifestation Gifts

The word "manifestation" is "phanerosis" in Greek, which means "shining forth" or "flashing forth." It is the Holy Spirit shining forth through us. These are temporary releases of God's knowledge, wisdom, or power through the Holy Spirit. In the next three verses of the passage, Paul lists nine of these gifts or manifestations.

For to one is given the word of wisdom through the Spirit, and to another the word of knowledge according to the same Spirit; to another faith by the same Spirit, and to another gifts of healing by the one Spirit, and to another the effecting of miracles, and to another prophecy, and to another the distinguishing of spirits, to another various kinds of tongues, and to another the interpretation of tongues.
- 1 Corinthians 12:8-10

These are nine expressions of God's knowledge, wisdom, and power operating through human vessels. Some have suggested that we group these gifts into three categories that correspond to the human body, since we are the Body of Christ. These categories are: eye gifts, hand gifts, and mouth gifts. Each addresses a different aspect of the Holy Spirit's ministry through Christ's spiritual Body which is the Church.

Eye Gifts:

The eye gifts are supernatural expressions of God's seeing and knowing. God is omniscient, and there is nothing that is hidden from Him. When the Holy Spirit gives one of these eye gifts through us, it is a manifestation of this aspect of God's character. They allow us to know something that we otherwise would not know and to see a situation as only God can see it.

Word of Wisdom: This is the first gift mentioned in the passage, and what it means is simple–God gives an individual His wisdom for a situation. Only God knows all the facts and only He can see the end even from the beginning. Only He has perfect understanding. A word of wisdom is when He shares His understanding with us so we might know what to do.

For example, years ago when our church was just beginning and still very small, I could not take a salary that was nearly large enough to provide for my family. I didn't know what to do. I knew that I was called to plant this church, but I also knew that God's Word is clear about a man's responsibility to provide for his family. What was I to do? One day, in prayer, I got a very clear picture of a yellow taxicab in my mind. Now the idea of driving a cab had never before entered into my mind. I had probably ridden in a cab maybe twice in my life. The concept was so strange to me that I tried several more closed doors before I looked into taxi driving.

What I discovered was that driving a taxi was the perfect solution to my problem. I had total flexibility in my schedule. Depending on the needs of the ministry I could decide to drive or not drive at a moment's notice. As the church grew I could gradually cut down the days I drove. Plus I met people I would have never met otherwise which taught me invaluable lessons. Believe me, you meet all types in a taxi–from pimps and gangsters to CEOs and politicians. I learned to understand them all and how to minister to them. In the midst of my dilemma God had given me His wisdom of what I should do.

Word of Knowledge: This is when the Holy Spirit reveals something unknown to you but known to God. You might be talking with a friend when, all of a sudden, God reveals to you that they've been struggling with suicidal thoughts. Armed with this knowledge, you are able to pray for that person, talk with them about their secret struggle, and get them the help they need. Often during ministry time God reveals a physical ailment that someone in the service has. This often leads to the person being healed after receiving prayer.

Once I was burdened for a young man who had left our church and gone back to live on the streets. I prayed much for him but didn't know how to find him. One day I felt a leading to go to a certain block of a busy street about ten miles from my home. I parked and began to walk up the street. Almost immediately I saw this young man sitting on a doorstep and was able to talk and minister to him. Although I did not know where this young man was, God did, and He shared His knowledge with me.

Discerning of Spirits: This gift allows us to recognize the presence and often the nature of a demonic spirit operating in a situation. This gift often manifests during a counseling or deliverance time. With this understanding, we can minister more effectively to set people free.

One time my friend, Michell, who is one of our counseling pastors, was counseling a man who said he was a Christian. As the man spoke, a strong impression came upon my friend that the man wasn't saved. Then a strong impression of the word "confusion" came to him. Michell's wife was also sitting in the session, so he leaned over and told her what he was experiencing. He asked her if she was getting anything, and she told him that she was having a vision of the man with a vulture sitting on his head with its claws going into the man's brain. Together they led the man to the Lord and cast out a spirit of confusion.

With all of these eye gifts, the Holy Spirit is communicating with us. He can do this in any way He chooses—for instance, sometimes people see a picture in their mind, get a mental impression, experience a physical sensation, have a dream, experience a memory flash into their mind, or just have a feeling. The method of God's communication isn't important. What is important is the information being given to us and that we act on it so we can see God's result. For the sake of clarity I have used dramatic examples to illustrate the reality of these gifts, but much more often these gifts come to us in more subtle ways. We need to develop sensitivity to the Holy Spirit to hear His gentle promptings and have the courage to act on them.

Hand Gifts:

Hand gifts are the works of God's power, which release His ability into human need. God is omnipotent, which means that nothing is beyond His power and ability. As eye gifts allow us to know something we otherwise wouldn't know, hand gifts allow us to do something we otherwise couldn't do.

Gifts of Healing: While God uses doctors, medicine, diet, and ongoing prayer to bring healing and health to people, gifts of healing are something different. These are immediate manifestations (a "flashing forth") of God's healing power in which healing is accomplished without the need of any additional medical help. These healings are usually accompanied by immediate relief of the effects or symptoms of the illness or impairment. Often, there is a physical sensation such as heat or tingling when healing is taking place. However, sometimes the evidence that a healing has taken place must wait upon something like a blood test or an ultrasound picture. But in each case the healing is a result of a direct encounter with the healing power of the Holy Spirit.

These are perhaps the best understood of the manifestation gifts. Many of us have experienced a healing or know someone who has. Because our church prays faithfully for those needing healing, we have seen many, many healings—a number of them quite spectacular. We have seen tumors disappear, broken bones healed, hearing restored to deaf ears, ruptured disks repaired, epileptics healed, etc.

I have prayed for sick people who have been healed and I myself have received healing through the prayers of others. When I was a young man, I had a chronic problem with tonsillitis. I would lose several weeks in bed every year to this condition. One day when I was sick in bed, a young man that I was mentoring came to pray for me. I felt miserable and didn't really want any company, but when he prayed for me, I felt heat in my throat and tonsils. Immediately, all swelling and pain went away. My fever was gone, and I was fully restored. It has been many years since I have had any problems with my tonsils.

Healing was an important part of Jesus' ministry. It should be an important part of any church's ministry as well. Anyone can be used by God to bring an immediate gift of healing to someone. The more we will pray, the more healings we will see. We will talk more about the subject of healing in a later chapter.

Miracles: These are extraordinary acts of God which defy natural laws and cause people to wonder and be in awe. Miracles are practical and solve a specific need; they are not simply fruitless, ostentatious displays. Of all the gifts, these are by far the rarest. People often label things which appear to be highly unlikely coincidences as miracles. God may have indeed orchestrated those "coincidences," but a miracle is more than that. **In order for something to be a miracle, it must violate a law of nature or physics.** When Jesus multiplied the loaves and fishes, walked on water, turned water into wine, and raised Lazarus from the dead, these were miracles.

I was blessed to witness a miracle years ago when Jesus multiplied money in a locked room in the same way that He multiplied the loaves so long ago. While we were away at seminary in Iowa, my brother Dave and I founded an independent parachurch organization dedicated to reaching young people in high school and college. We believed that God spoke to us about putting together a particular Christian event. Although we didn't have sufficient money to pay for it, we believed that God would supply the necessary funds through a free will offering taken at the event.

After the event was over and everyone had gone home, we took the offering money back to our apartment to count it. We counted all the checks and folding money and then did a quick estimate of the change. We were devastated to learn that we only had half as much as we needed. The next morning we went to pick up our special guest minister to take him to the airport. We told him that we could not pay him what we had promised. We were crushed. We assured him that we would get the money somehow and send it along later. The guest artist was very gracious and told us that he sensed that God was really in the event and for us not to worry about the money. We assured him that we really were going to send the money to him later when we could find a way. We put him on the plane and went back home.

We decided that we would recount the money exactly so we could fill out a deposit slip. This time when we counted, we had almost exactly twice the amount of the previous night–just enough to cover all the costs. We had not found any uncounted money nor had we missed any large checks. The building we lived in had a locked door to the street and another locked door to get into our apartment, so it wasn't possible that anyone added the money. It took us a while to get over the shock and admit that there was no possible explanation other than God had multiplied the money. I don't know if God was testing us or testing the guest minister. I know that some will have a hard time accepting this, but I only report what I saw with my own eyes.

Faith: This is something different than the gift of faith by which we gain salvation.[44] It is more than just developing strong faith by walking with the Lord. This is instead a deposit of faith or a burst of confidence given by God for a specific occasion, need, or task. It can empower us to act

---

[44] Ephesians 2:8; Acts 11:18

boldly in the face of an overwhelming obstacle, certain that God will intervene. It can sustain us and give us the drive and encouragement to see the Lord's work through great delays and difficulties to the end. Think of Moses standing before the Red Sea and raising up his staff to part it, Elijah challenging the prophets of Baal, Peter standing up on the day of Pentecost to preach to those who had recently crucified Jesus, or Peter telling Tabitha to rise from the dead.

I experienced this in a powerful way when the Lord gave me the idea to start our Youth Venture Teen Centers, a ministry that has helped thousands of young people get off destructive paths and onto a good one. When I first had the idea, we didn't have the money, experience, staff, or influence to make something so audacious happen. Many people said I was being foolish, but I was so filled with God's faith whenever I would think of this ministry that I knew God was behind it and would bring it to pass. That burst of faith enabled us to carry out the vision, and God has blessed it–as I knew He would.

Mouth Gifts:

Mouth gifts are manifestations of God's speaking. His words give life. Mouth gifts allow us to speak messages from God.

Prophecy: Prophecy as a manifestation gift is a specific revelation of God's will concerning a particular person, group, or situation. It can refer to the future or the present.[45] These prophetic words give comfort, encouragement, and confirmation of God's direction. Many times I have seen prophecies give great courage to people. I have received prophecies from others that have made a profound difference in my life and ministry.

Many years ago, I dropped out of ministry absolutely discouraged and dejected. I was seriously struggling with the question of whether God had ever called me to be a pastor. As a result, I was looking for another career direction. One night, I went to a meeting at a church I had never been to before. They had a traveling prophetic minister named Marc Dupont[46] whom I had never met or even heard of. Towards the end of the meeting, he called me out of the crowd and prophesied that God had called me into the ministry and even prophesied some of the ways that God was going to use me in the future. God used that prophecy to assure me and relaunch me, and His words came to pass just as He said.

Another time, a few years later, my brother Dave and I had started two separate churches which were both struggling. We had both been praying about the possibility of bringing those two churches together. One day someone told us they had a vision of two small, struggling plants being intertwined together that grew until it became a great tree. God used that prophecy to confirm His direction to us. That new church that we began 33 years ago was Foothills Christian Church, a church we both still pastor today that has had a powerful, worldwide impact.

---

[45] Prophecy, in this sense, is distinguished from prophecy as listed in Romans 12, which refers to a more general declaration of God's truth, which can be found in His Word and thus cultivated as a discipline. We will look at this in the next chapter.

[46] The founder of Mantle of Praise Ministries, who travels internationally with a prophetic and healing ministry. Today, he is on staff at our church.

Tongues: Tongues is a spiritual language that allows you to speak to God during prayer and worship beyond the limits of your knowledge or understanding. It allows the Holy Spirit to put unknown words in you so that your spirit can continue to talk to God beyond the limits of your mind.[47] You can engage tongues in this way in prayer and worship whenever you want to, and it can minister to you powerfully.[48] It can be a powerful aid. However, I believe that the manifestation gift of tongues spoken of here is different. Rather than you speaking to God in prayer, this is God speaking to men through the unknown language of your tongue. Therefore, it must be linked with the next gift, the interpretation of tongues, for it to be beneficial to others in a public setting.[49] God does not give this manifestation gift without also sending an interpretation. If it is not interpreted, then it is out of order and will not edify those gathered. A message from God in tongues is accompanied with the understanding that this is a message for the whole group, in the same way that someone discerns he has a prophecy.

Interpretation of Tongues: The interpretation of tongues is the ability to translate a message spoken through the gift of tongues. It allows one to translate an otherwise unintelligible message for the spiritual benefit of those who are gathered. An interpretation of tongues is discerned in the same way as when you receive a prophecy: You have a clear conviction that the Holy Spirit wants to speak through you. If the interpretation is genuine, then the proof of it is that all those who are gathered will be edified.

---

[47] 1 Corinthians 14:2,14; Romans 8:26
[48] 1 Corinthians 14:4
[49] 1 Corinthians 14:27-28

All of these nine gifts are God's compassionate hand extended to people in need. They flow through imperfect but available people. Remember, all of these gifts are referred to as "manifestations." They are not spiritual abilities which a person can exercise at will but rather each one is a "shining forth" of the Holy Spirit's power, knowledge, or wisdom among us. No one possesses a manifestation gift; they are individual events that the Holy Spirit dispenses as He chooses.

But one and the same Spirit works all these things, distributing to each one individually just as He wills.
- 1 Corinthians 12:11

These manifestations can flow through any Christian, but they are not evenly distributed among them. The Holy Spirit distributes these manifestations according to God's wisdom and strategy, and often according to God's callings and appointments in the Church. We will look at this in more detail in the next chapter, where we examine another list of spiritual gifts quite different from the one we have been studying. This list contains what I call the "function gifts," which will also help us understand how the Holy Spirit distributes the manifestation gifts we have discussed in this chapter.

Chapter 5

Spiritual Gifts Part II: The Function Gifts

A Second List of Gifts of the Spirit

In Romans 12 we encounter a second list of seven spiritual gifts which even a cursory reading reveals are quite different from the list in 1 Corinthians 12.

Let's look at the passage:

> *Since we have gifts that differ according to the grace given to us, each of us is to exercise them accordingly: if prophecy, according to the proportion of his faith; if service, in his serving; or he who teaches, in his teaching; or he who exhorts, in his exhortation; he who gives, with liberality; he who leads, with diligence; he who shows mercy, with cheerfulness.*
> *- Romans 12:6-8*

The first thing we notice in the above passage is that this list is almost completely different from the list in 1 Corinthians 12. There is only one gift that appears in both: the gift of prophecy (more on this later).

The second very important thing we notice is that the word "manifestation," which is key in understanding the first list, doesn't appear anywhere in this chapter.[50] Instead the key word to understanding this list appears two verses earlier. It is the word "function."

For just as we have many members in one body and all the members do not have the same function, so we, who are many, are one body in Christ, and individually members one of another.   - Romans 12:4-5

The word "function" refers to how a person functions in the Body of Christ—that is what we are specifically equipped and called to do. One list is characterized by the word "manifestations" and the other by the word "function." Manifestation gifts are occasional displays of God's power and knowledge while function gifts refer to our role in the Body. Failure to understand this important difference leads to confusion.

Another important indicator that these lists refer to very different types of gifts is contained in verse 6, where we read, "since we have gifts that differ...[let us] exercise them accordingly." In 1 Corinthians 12 we read that the Holy Spirit distributes the manifestations as He wills, but here we read that we have or possess these gifts and are responsible to be good stewards of them.[51] In other words, I may possess the gift of teaching or of serving,[52] but I cannot possess the gift of miracles or healing.[53] These function gifts are our job descriptions in the Body of Christ.

Let's look at this list of gifts:

---

50 1 Corinthians 12:7
51 1 Corinthians 12:7, 11
52 Romans 12
53 1 Corinthians 12

Prophecy: This first gift is the only one that appears in both lists. This is because the Greek word that we translate as "prophecy" has a very broad meaning. The word "prophetia" literally means "to speak forth," and it refers to speaking forth the mind and counsel of God. This can refer to a revelation of something future or previously unknown, such as in 1 Corinthians 12, or it can refer more broadly to simply proclaiming God's Word. Here it is used in its broader sense of a calling or job description.

This gift refers to all who are burdened and gifted to proclaim God's "now" Word to others. Prophetic preaching addresses the pressing needs of the hour with a clear word from God, usually using the scriptures. It is different from the gift of teaching, which is the systematic exposition of unchanging biblical principles and doctrine. The *function* gift of prophecy gives God's perspective and direction concerning current issues in an ever-changing culture. The 20th century Swiss theologian Karl Barth is generally credited with the saying, "One should preach with the Bible in one hand and the newspaper in the other." This is unlike the *manifestation* gift of prophecy, which is distributed on an as-needed basis by the Holy Spirit. Rather, this function gift is an ability given by the Holy Spirit that abides in the individual. Many pastors have this gift as well as most prophets.

Service: This gift is the God-given motivation and ability to meet practical needs and thereby build up the Body of Christ. People with this gift often serve by making meals, fixing cars for those in need, driving buses, ushering, doing maintenance, counting offerings, repairing homes for single moms, watching other people's kids, and in many other ways. All of us need to serve, but these people are the most willing, have the greatest strength and patience in serving, and derive the most joy from it. This is one of the most frequently given gifts because there is so much service that needs to be done.

Teaching: This is the ability to help people understand and make practical application of God's Word in their lives. These people's highest motivation is to help prepare people to succeed by helping them understand God's principles. They are systematic thinkers who love digging deep in the Bible.

Exhortation: This is the ability to encourage others to trust and obey God. Exhortation is a much-needed gift because there are many fearful and discouraged people who can fall easily into temptation and defeat; although they may know God's will, they lack the courage and motivation to fully obey and therefore fall short of God's full blessing. People with the gift of exhortation can stimulate others to greater obedience and good works. They look past people's failings and see the best in them. They effectively encourage people to live at a higher level. These people are often the most effective at evangelism.

Giving: This is the motivation and ability to give generously and sacrificially with great joy. These are God's trusted stewards that He often entrusts much financial blessing to. They derive great joy from giving and do not seek recognition for their generosity. Their reward is pleasing the Lord. Without this gift, much of the outreach of the Church could not happen.

Leadership: This is the ability to recognize people's gifting and to organize and supervise them to accomplish God's goals. Nothing much will happen that is significant and lasting unless these people are in place. Many who are gifted as pastors or teachers are not gifted as leaders. This is one reason why team ministry is so important and why churches must collaborate together. Ezra was a tremendous teacher of God's Word and was able to prepare the people, but it was not until the arrival of Nehemiah, who was strongly gifted as a leader, that Jerusalem was rebuilt.

Showing Mercy: This is the motivation and ability to reveal God's compassion to the downcast and suffering. These people are drawn to those who are hurting, have suffered loss, are sick, housebound, or are in some other sort of need. They are able to bring healing and hope by demonstrating and embodying God's mercy. This is a gift God gives to many people because there are so many hurting people.

Sometimes people refer to this list as the "motivational gifts" because they help motivate us to focus on different aspects of ministry. God gives us a measure of His compassion and vision for those who would benefit from our gift. When we are operating in our area of gifting, we receive special grace and joy. When you are employing your gift, you leave feeling energized rather than fatigued and depleted. For instance, while all of us are called to serve and show mercy when a need is before us, those who are gifted in these areas often get there ahead of us, are especially useful, and finish feeling very joyful.

Releasing Your Gift

These seven gifts all have something in common: We must employ them in order to release them. They are activities that you can choose to engage and grow in. You can become powerful and highly effective in each of them. In fact, God instructs us to do so when He says, "exercise them accordingly."[54] For instance, you can become more effective as a teacher by studying and making the most of the opportunities to teach that you are given. Likewise, you can learn to excel at giving, at leadership, at serving, at encouraging, at proclaiming truth, and at showing mercy. God tells us that we must be good stewards and employ our gift for the good of the Body.

As each one has received a special gift, employ it in serving one another as good stewards of the manifold grace of God
-1 Peter 4:10

The gift spoken of here is most likely one of those listed in Romans 12 since we are told that we have "received" it and must be "good stewards" by using or "employing" it. Unfortunately, we have an unemployment problem in the Church—that is we have many Christians who are not employing their gifts. This results in a supply shortage in the Church. If every gift is employed, then every need can be met, for God has given a sufficient supply.

Paul reminds us that every Christian has been given a valuable and needed gift. This means that if you do not serve with your gift, then what you could supply will

---

[54] Romans 12:6

be missing. The Church will suffer from its loss. Now you know that what you have long suspected is true—you really are God's gift to the world.

As you have read this chapter, you may have already recognized what your function gift is. If you are unsure, talk to your pastor or a mature Christian who knows you well. They have probably already noticed your area of gifting. The more you get involved in ministering to others, the more your area of gifting will become apparent.

Peter says that these gifts express the "manifold" or many forms of God's grace. The Greek word used here, "poikiols," literally means "many-colored." God's grace comes to us in many different forms. The members of a church are a tapestry of many different colors, and together they can supply for every need. You are very valuable, and what God has given you to share is vitally needed. Never let disappointments or misunderstandings make you doubt that. Never just sit on the bench when you are desperately needed in the game.

The Body of Christ is an amazing depository of God's riches. Within all of its members lay a vast potential to change the world. A passage in 1 Corinthians gives us further insight into the wonderful mystery that is the Church, by comparing it to a human body.

The Interdependency of the Body

For the body is not one member, but many. If the foot says, "Because I am not a hand, I am not a part of the body," it is not for this reason any the less a part of the body. And if the ear says, "Because I am not an eye, I am not a part of the body," it is not for this reason any the less a part of the body. If the whole body were an eye, where would the hearing

be? If the whole were hearing, where would the sense of smell be? But now God has placed the members, each one of them, in the body, just as He desired. If they were all one member, where would the body be? But now there are many members, but one body. And the eye cannot say to the hand, "I have no need of you"; or again the head to the feet, "I have no need of you." ...But God has so composed the body, giving more abundant honor to that member which lacked, so that there may be no division in the body, but that the members may have the same care for one another. And if one member suffers, all the members suffer with it; if one member is honored, all the members rejoice with it. Now you are Christ's body, and individually members of it.
- 1 Corinthians 12:14-21, 24-27

Just as Jesus had a physical body through which He acted when He walked the earth, He now has a spiritual Body through which He continues to operate. **God, in His wisdom, has given Christ's spiritual Body the same design concepts He gave to our physical bodies.**

Diversity of Function: In the human body there are different parts to perform different functions. Each of these parts is necessary. All are important. It is the same with Christ's Body, the Church.

Specialization: Each of the parts of the human body is wonderfully designed to accomplish its purpose. Each part plays its role so the body can function at peak health and efficiency. So also in the Church. God equips and empowers each member to be fruitful in his or her role. When you function in your role, you are powerful! Though some members might have greater visibility, they are not more important. They are not equipped as you are to fulfil your role. You are needed.

Interdependence: The eye cannot see if the nerve cell does not carry the electrical impulse to the brain. The respiratory system and the circulatory system must work together for the muscles to get their oxygen. In the same way, a big-name evangelist can't have a huge altar call without an army of other gifted people doing their jobs. Think of how many different gifts it takes to operate even a typical weekend service. Consider how many different gifts must work together to reach, evangelize, disciple, encourage, comfort, equip, and care for the lost in our communities (and their children).

Diversity of function, specialization, and interdependence are God-given keys to kingdom growth. Consider what specialization has brought to our modern world. Whether it's medicine, science, industry, education, technology, or any other field, we make far greater and faster progress when people specialize. Modern society has benefited greatly from discovering God's design. God, the designer, has put these concepts of diversity of function, specialization, and interdependence into everything He has created. We find it everywhere from single cell organisms to elephants. It's also in God's design for marriage, the family, and the Church.

God makes each of us specialists so that there will be greater progress in His kingdom spreading across the earth. When we specialize we become more focused and grow dramatically in our skill and fruitfulness. Understanding this also helps us understand why some people seem to be conduits of many manifestation gifts while others seldom experience them.

Function Gifts and Manifestation Gifts are Interrelated

Manifestation gifts are often like tools that people need as they operate in their function gifts. That's why certain manifestation gifts seem to cluster around certain function gifts. For instance, it's not surprising that a person who has the gift of exhortation and is called to evangelism would more often receive the manifestation gift (tool) of healing, than, say, the one whose gift is service. Healing is often an important part of someone coming to Christ. In the same way, one who has the role of leadership would more often receive the manifestation gift of a word of wisdom than one who has the gift of exhorter/evangelist. This makes sense, and it is what we find to be true.

In the same way, we see a connection between certain fivefold ministries and certain manifestation gifts.[55] Prophets and evangelists see the most manifestations since such gifts serve to authenticate the gospel message being preached and to encourage people to listen to the

---

[55] This is a third list of gifts in the New Testament in Ephesians 4:7-13. This list is altogether different from the ones that we have been studying. These gifts are official ministries in the Church and the people who Jesus appoints to them. Apostles, prophets, evangelists, pastors and teachers are sometimes referred to as the "fivefold ministry gifts" or the "ascension gifts" because Christ gave them to the Church after He ascended (v.8). It is noteworthy that: The manifestation gifts are said to be given by the Holy Spirit (1 Corinthians 12:4, 11), the function gifts by God (Romans 12:3,6a), and the fivefold ministry gifts by Jesus (Ephesians 4:7-11). These are the leaders God raises up to lead and govern His Church.

These are three different lists of gifts given by the three members of the Trinity for separate but complimentary purposes to accomplish God's great goal.

prophecies being spoken. In the same way, a pastor might need words of knowledge to reveal the hidden difficulties that are hindering someone they are counseling from moving forward.

There is a widespread teaching in some circles that all Christians should expect to be able to move equally in all the gifts. I believe this is wrong. While it is true that any believer can display any manifestation gift if the Holy Spirit wills it, this teaching does not bear in mind God's biblical principles of diversity of function and specialization in the Body. It has, I believe, led to much confusion, discouragement, frustration, and even self-deception among God's people.

Take the person who genuinely wants to be fruitful for Jesus and experience the great manifestations that a well-known prophet or evangelists talks about. They might go from conference to conference and seminar to seminar hoping to be able to walk in everything that they heard about. After all, they have been told that they can and should. But after much sincere trying, they still find that they do not seem to be used much in these manifestation gifts. What are they to make of it? Perhaps they begin to question themselves. "What's wrong with me? I have done everything they said. Maybe I don't have enough faith, or maybe I am not favored by God." Or perhaps they will conclude that all of this spiritual gifts stuff isn't true and walk away from it–maybe even away from the Church. On the other hand, they may go the route that some have taken and begin to think that every inward impression must be from the Holy Spirit. Or, even worse yet, in their confusion and zeal they may begin to accept manifestations from deceiving spirits.

All this confusion is unnecessary if people understand their role and gift in the Body. We need to understand that every gift is important and to be equally honored. Every function gift is equally necessary if the Body of Christ is to make progress. It is foolish for any of us to wish that we had a different gift than the one our heavenly Father, in His love and wisdom, has given us.

> *For by one Spirit we were all baptized into one body, whether Jews or Greeks, whether slaves or free, and we were all made to drink of one Spirit. For the body is not one member, but many... If the whole body were an eye, where would the hearing be? If the whole were hearing, where would the sense of smell be? But now God has placed the members, each one of them, in the body, just as He desired.*
> *- 1 Corinthians 12:13-14, 17-18*

God has carefully placed us in the Body. The word translated "placed" is the Greek word "tithemi," which can also be translated as "set," "appoint," or "assign." We are appointed by God to our ministry gift, assigned our role, and carefully set into the Body so that it can function effectively and powerfully. Every part is essential. Whether you are a hand or an eye or a liver, you are important and necessary.

It is foolish to ask which gift is best. The best gift is the one that is needed at the moment. If your car is broken down on the side of the road, do you want someone equipped and motivated with a gift of service or do you want someone to preach or prophesy to your car? This may seem like a silly illustration, but it shows the importance of every gift. Rightly understanding spiritual gifts is an important key to being fruitful and living an overcoming life. One more important element is developing spiritual discernment, which we will look at in the following chapter.

Chapter 6

Growing in Spiritual Discernment

But I fear, lest somehow, as the serpent deceived Eve by his craftiness, so your minds may be corrupted from the simplicity that is in Christ. For if He who comes preaches another Jesus whom we have not preached, or if you receive a different spirit which you have not received, or a different gospel which you have not accepted—you may well put up with it!
- 2 Corinthians 11:3-4 NKJV

The devil is a master counterfeiter. We learned in chapter 4 that anything that is of value will be counterfeited, and so it is. In the above passage we learn that the devil offers:

- **A different spirit** than the Holy Spirit
- **A different Jesus** than the One the apostles proclaimed
- **A different gospel** than the one the apostles preached

The early Church was acutely aware of their need to be alert to spiritual deception. The New Testament warns of false, distorted gospels being preached,[56] of false prophets,[57] of false apostles,[58] of deceitful angels bringing different

---

[56] Galatians 1:6-7
[57] Matthew 7:15; 1 John 4:1
[58] 2 Corinthians 11:13

gospels,[59] of lying demons bringing false doctrines,[60] and even Satan disguising himself as an angel of light.[61] Some in the modern Church seem careless of such dangers.

Now please understand me, our heavenly Father certainly does not want us to live in fear of Satan or of being deceived. Jesus clearly taught us that we should be confident that if we ask God for His Holy Spirit, He will give the Holy Spirit to us, not some counterfeit.[62] We should be continually asking for fresh infillings and eagerly desiring spiritual gifts.[63] We can trust the Holy Spirit to wisely distribute His gifts among us.[64] We can trust the Holy Spirit to come to our aid and equip us and teach us what to say when we face danger and difficulties.[65]

However, this does not mean that we can carelessly disregard the warnings God has given us. If people remain humble and teachable, then they can trust that God will lead them away from spiritual deception and keep them in the truth. But when people fail to test everything by Scripture and in pride reject the counsel of pastors and leaders, then they can rush headlong into spiritual error and bondage. It seems that increasing numbers are making this mistake in our day. For this reason I feel the need to write about spiritual deception and how to avoid it. Let's begin our study at the beginning.

---

[59] Galatians 1:8
[60] 1 Timothy 4:1
[61] 2 Corinthians 11:14
[62] Luke 11: 9-13
[63] 1 Corinthians 14:1
[64] 1 Corinthians 12:7-11
[65] Luke 12:11-12

In the Garden

True religion and spiritual deception began all the way back in the Garden of Eden. We can trace their beginnings to the first three chapters of Genesis. We find the source of true religion in the first chapter. In just three verses (Genesis 1:27-29), God tells us our identity, purpose, and our proper relationship to all things. It is the foundation of true religion.

God gives us **our identity:**

God created man in His own image, in the image of God He created him; male and female He created them.
- Genesis 1:27

Who am I? I am created in the image of Another. I will never understand myself until I grasp this truth. I was not created for my own pleasure but for His. That is why living for my own pleasure is so unsatisfying and ends in failure. He created me in His image so that I could relate to Him and know Him, and also so I could reflect His glory. He also created each of us as one of two different sexual beings, each one with a unique design and separate functions. All this forms the basis of our identity.

He gave us **our purpose:**

God blessed them; and God said to them, "Be fruitful and multiply; and fill the earth and subdue it; and rule over the fish of the sea and over the birds of the sky and over every living thing that moves on the earth."   - Genesis 1:28

What is my purpose? Why am I here? This verse tells us that our purpose is to rule under God and bring about His purposes through following His directives and rules. The Bible tells us that God placed Adam and Eve in the Garden of Eden to cultivate and guard it.[66] Our purpose is to nurture and extend the boundaries of God's garden of blessings and goodness across the earth. I find meaning in life as I live to accomplish His will. It is what I was made for.

He explained **our relationship with the things of this life:**

Then God said, "Behold, I have given you every plant yielding seed that is on the surface of all the earth, and every tree which has fruit yielding seed; it shall be for food for you."
- Genesis 1:29

Everything belongs to God because He created everything. He shares His things with us as gifts to use. He supplies our every need. He gives generously to those that are His so we need not fear.[67] However, since He is the owner of everything, He alone determines how His gifts are to be used. He sets limits. For instance, He gave them all the fruit trees for food except He set one aside and forbade them from eating of it.[68]

This is true religion and the worldview which leads to abundant living. By it we understand who we are, what our purpose is, what we've been given, and how to properly use it to achieve success and happiness. This is God's revealed religion.

---

[66] Genesis 2:15
[67] Matthew 6:25-33
[68] Genesis 2:16-17

Unfortunately, as we know, this was not the end of the story. There was a deceiver in the Garden who introduced a counterfeit religion. We are introduced to this false religion in Genesis 3.

Deception

> *Now the serpent was more crafty than any beast of the field which the Lord God had made. And he said to the woman, "Indeed, has God said, 'You shall not eat from any tree of the garden'?" The woman said to the serpent, "From the fruit of the trees of the garden we may eat; but from the fruit of the tree which is in the middle of the garden, God has said, 'You shall not eat from it or touch it, or you will die.'" The serpent said to the woman, "You surely will not die!"*
> *- Genesis 3:1-4*

Eve had a powerful spiritual encounter in this passage, but it wasn't with God; it was with Satan. God's Spirit wasn't the only spirit that had access to the Garden. Satan was present even in that ideal environment. This is an important lesson. The Holy Spirit isn't the only spirit that wants to approach us and even instruct us. Let's look at how Satan deceived Eve. He follows the same three-step process to deceive us today.

First, the serpent begins by misrepresenting God's Word, as though God had forbidden all the trees. When Eve responds that it is only one tree that they are forbidden from, the serpent essentially says to her, "Listen, if the other trees won't kill you, then neither will this one that God has forbidden you. It is silly to think that this one particular tree is any different from the rest. God is merely placing an unreasonable restriction on you and your happiness." He attempts to separate her from God's Word and get her to rely on her own reasoning. He presents God's Word as an unfair restriction. This is always the first step in Satan's plan to lead us into deception. He attempts to diminish our reliance on God's Word so we can be led astray.

Once the devil had sidestepped God's Word, look what he does next:

> *For God knows that in the day you eat from it your eyes will be opened, and you will be like God, knowing good and evil.*
> *- Genesis 3:5*

Here Satan introduces the second step into spiritual deception: Turning inward to elevate subjective experience above God's Word. He tells her that by this act of eating the forbidden fruit, she can receive a spiritual impartation to know truth by subjective inner impression. She will no longer need any objective standards outside herself.

One further aspect of "being like God" and knowing good and evil directly is that one need no longer listen to any spiritual authority. Satan approached Eve apart from her husband Adam, who had been created first and had given Eve her name.

This is the third step, separating people from the spiritual authorities that God has placed in their lives. Like every predator in nature, Satan seeks to cut us off from the herd and isolate us so we can be more easily devoured.[69] The Bible tells us that pastors and leaders, "*keep watch over your soul as those who will have to give an account.*"[70]

---

[69] 1 Peter 5:8
[70] Hebrews 13:17; see also Acts 20:28

Satan seeks to separate us from our leaders by appealing to our pride, telling us that we are now more advanced than they are. He does this so that we will not receive their warnings or correction but now can be swayed by mystical experiences that he is only too happy to supply.

You almost always see this same threefold pattern in anyone who goes into spiritual/mystical deception.

- First, their reliance on the Bible is diminished. They read it less and it holds less influence in their lives. They lose their appetite for biblical expository teaching, and in the meetings they now attend, Bible teaching does not play a central role. In its place there are lots of fantastic claims and anecdotal stories of supposed spiritual experiences that they or someone else has had.
- Next, those on this path to deception begin to accept all spiritual experiences uncritically, no matter how little scriptural support there is for them.
- Finally, they drift away from their former Christian friends and spiritual leaders.

You quite likely know people who have followed this pattern. You may want to take a moment and evaluate how you are doing in these three areas.

The Two Religions

There are two basic types of religion in the world today. The first is found in Genesis 1. It descends to us from heaven. I call it "**Prophetic/Biblical Religion**" because it is based on God speaking to us. It is the self-revelation of

God primarily communicated to us by language or words.[71] God is high above all and is only truly known because He has revealed Himself through chosen messengers, such as prophets and apostles, and His greatest self-revelation in Jesus Christ. This self-revelation is recorded in the Bible.

I call the second religion **Pagan/Mystical**. It promises that spiritual transcendence or the divine life can be gained by earthly and human practices, such as when Eve ate the apple. Whereas Prophetic/Biblical Religion requires God descending to us, mysticism promises that we can ascend to God. It is the attempt to know truth by inward, mystical encounters. The idea is that we ascend to God (or the spirit world, or higher planes of reality) through learning techniques and practices such as meditation, chanting, altered states of consciousness, etc. It is man reaching up to heaven. It is the heart of Satan's spiritual deception. It was the delusion which led Satan to rebel in heaven.[72]

We meet these two religious streams in the first three chapters of Genesis. From there they flow down throughout history to the present day. Judaism and Christianity represent Prophetic/Biblical Religion. Islam would be grouped here as well since it is a later corruption of Judaism and Christianity.[73] Virtually all other religions are Pagan/Mystical. Even Judaism and Islam have mystical corruptions. In Judaism it is known as Kabala, and in Islam as Sufism. These corruptions have more in common with mysticism than they do with the two religions from which they arose. In the same way, mysticism found a place

---

[71] 1 Corinthians 2:12-13; 2 Timothy 3:16-17

[72] Isaiah 14:12-15

[73] Islam arose in the Middle East almost six centuries after Christianity. Judaism and Christianity were the dominant religions in the area, and Mohammad borrowed heavily from them and from Bible history.

among early Christians. The New Testament witnesses to the battle the early Church had with this influence. Its most common form was an early form of the heresy of Gnosticism.[74] These ideas have swept back into the Church since the rise of New Age religions in the West. We read in 2 Corinthians 11:3-4 that the same deceiving spirit which successfully deceived Eve in the Garden is still trying to deceive believers today. Let's go over some concrete ways to discern error and avoid spiritual deception.

The first and most basic test is this: Does this activity involve the descent of God to us or our ascent to Him and the heavenly realm? In Prophetic/Biblical Religion, the initiative is always with God. We can pray, call out, and lift our voices in worship, but we must wait on God to respond and take the initiative to answer us or meet with us. The biblical record and our own common experience demonstrates that God often keeps us waiting for answers and breakthroughs. While we wait for God to answer us, we trust and encourage ourselves in what He has already said and promised in the Bible. This waiting is a very challenging and stretching aspect of the Christian life. It is tempting to wish there were shortcuts. And it is this wish that gives Satan his opportunity.

Satan tells us that we don't have to wait, that the initiative lies with us. He told Eve that if she would take the initiative and eat the forbidden fruit, she would gain heightened spiritual awareness. It was, of course, a very costly deception. Satan no longer has forbidden fruit to offer us but instead tells us that we can gain heightened

---

[74] For instance, it is generally recognized that such books as the Letter to the Colossians, 1 John, and 1 Corinthians were partially written to battle this influence.

spiritual awareness through turning inward and practicing such techniques as meditation, chanting, using drugs, or receiving spiritual transfer (impartation/activation) from some guru, religious leader, spirit guide, or angelic being. We may not always recognize, at first glance, the forms these practices take today.

Many practices now becoming popular in some wings of the Church have been practiced for centuries in eastern religions. These New Age practices have entered the evangelical Church because the temptation to find spiritual shortcuts and transcend the need to wait upon God is a strong one.

Consider some things I have heard taught in so-called Christian conferences and seminars:

Deceptive Practices in the Church Today

Recently, I saw a "revival" meeting on the internet where the popular leader told the attendees to "reach up with your hands into the heavenly realm and pull down the glory." Of course, most of the compliant attendees attempted to do just that. I am sure that many were just caught up in the emotions of the moment. But consider how foolish is the idea that we can access God's glory merely by reaching up and pulling it down. This is mysticism, not prophetic religion.

Ten years ago, a "prophet-revivalist" by the name of Todd Bentley was holding meetings in Lakeland, Florida. The meetings drew international attention, and the nightly meetings were broadcast to the whole world. People began streaming to these meetings from all across America and the globe. A huge tent that could seat 10,000 people was filled to capacity many nights. Todd claimed that the secret to his ministry was that another well-known leader, Bob Jones, had sent his personal angel "Emma" to assist him. Many well-known leaders endorsed these meetings, and it was widely claimed that these meetings were going to usher in a great "end-times revival."

A friend greatly encouraged me to attend, and I agreed to go and see it for myself. Unknown to me, Todd had been removed from the leadership of these meetings the day before I arrived because it became known that he was abusing alcohol and was having an affair with one of his young female staffers. In his place, the meetings were being run by members of his ministry, "Fresh Fire."

The speaker that night taught us that we were created to live in both the physical and spiritual realms. Just as God had given us five physical senses so we could operate in the physical world, so He had given us five spiritual senses so we could operate in the spiritual world. As a result, we could learn to see, hear, taste, touch, and smell the spiritual world. He told us that through their "anointed prayers" we could activate these senses. Now, I am sure that to many people this sounded logical. They also offered seminars the next morning where people could be taught to spiritually ascend to heaven and *"see, hear and smell the aromas of heaven."* By now you can already discern that this is mysticism, not biblical Christianity. We do not have inborn abilities to see or smell heaven. Nor can we spiritually ascend into heaven whenever we desire.

While it is true that we have a spirit, we are not yet fully spiritual beings. Our newborn spirits are still wed to a physical body with its limitations.[75] We will not be fully functional spiritual beings until we are transformed upon

---

[75] 2 Corinthians 4:7, 16

our death or when Christ returns.[76] Not acknowledging our present limitations leads to exaggerated claims of spiritual experiences and powers. Sadly, the whole Todd Bentley episode is an alarming picture of the lack of discernment in some parts of the Church today.

Mystical Christianity often relies on radical and liberal views of the Bible in order to undermine our trust in biblical truth. As we saw in Genesis 3, the heart of this religion is turning inward to mystical/spiritual experiences. The same deceiving spirit that was successful with Eve in the Garden of Eden we find still trying to deceive believers in the New Testament.[77] There were many spiritual manifestations in the early Church, and believers were responsible to test them to see if they were actually from God.

Beloved, do not believe every spirit, but test the spirits to see whether they are from God, because many false prophets have gone out into the world. By this you know the Spirit of God: every spirit that confesses that Jesus Christ has come in the flesh is from God... We are from God; he who knows God listens to us; he who is not from God does not listen to us. By this we know the spirit of truth and the spirit of error.
- 1 John 4:1-2, 6

When John says, "He who knows God *listens to us,*" the "us" he is referring to are the chosen apostles of Jesus who gave us the New Testament doctrine. Any teaching that is

---

76 1 Corinthians 13:12-13; Philippians 3:20-21; 1 Corinthians 15:42-44; 51-53; 2 Corinthians 5:6-7
77 2 Corinthians 11:3

not in accordance with New Testament doctrine is not to be accepted.[78]

Questions to Ask in Discerning the Holy Spirit from Mystical Counterfeits

1. Who is God?

Biblical Religion teaches that God has revealed Himself both as a loving Father and as a righteous judge with moral laws that must be obeyed. We do not get to define God. He has defined Himself. He is a relational being, but He is also King of the Universe, so we must approach Him with awe, respect, and obedience.

Mystical Religion says that God is essentially power and love. It teaches that religion is an inward, subjective experience, and objective rules are not important. It leads to extreme views of grace and universalism as well as openness to unbiblical, alternative lifestyles. The ancient pagans would seek their gods for power, but there was no moral requirement. Wherever mysticism creeps into the Church, God's revelation of Himself and His standards are gradually replaced by more acceptable, current, secular and cultural views. Biblical teaching is either ignored or redefined to conform to modern views.

2. What Are Spiritual Gifts?

Biblical Religion teaches that spiritual gifts belong to the Holy Spirit, Who gives them when He wants to.[79] They are

---

[78] The Bible also teaches us that the writings of the OT prophets and authors are also to be used to discern true revelation from false revelation; see Isaiah 8:19-20.
[79] 1 Corinthians 12:7, 11

manifestations that come in His timing, not ours. We explored this in chapter 4.

Mystical Religion often speaks of gifts as though they are abilities that can be taught and developed. The idea is that we can walk in supernatural abilities all of the time if only we learn the right techniques or believe hard enough. While it is true that we should grow in becoming more accurate and fruitful with the manifestation gifts the Holy Spirit gives us, this is different from viewing them as special abilities we can learn and exercise at will.

For instance, I was present at a seminar where the leader had those attending mill about the room among each other and told them that when he blew the whistle they were to prophesy to whoever they found themselves standing next to. They were told that if they just started blessing the person, whatever came to their mind next would be a prophetic thought. It was explained by another leader in this way: God's thoughts toward each of His children are more than the sand on all of the seashores, and all we had to do was "reach up and grab one of His thoughts of that person and prophesy it to them." Now, there is no biblical warrant for this, and I think we can all see how this can lead to great misunderstanding and many spurious "prophesies."

3. What Is the Focus of the Spirit's Work Among Us?

Biblical Religion teaches that the Holy Spirit primarily convicts us of sin and our need for Jesus, leading to people getting saved, discipled, and growing in the faith.[80] Spiritual

---

[80] John 16:7-11

manifestations and experiences should therefore lead to greater humility, holiness, Christlikeness, and unity with the entire Body of Christ. The Holy Spirit was also given to glorify Christ.[81] But when the focus is regularly drawn to angels, exotic manifestations, and the "anointing" of the leader—all of which distract from a focus on Jesus—we have to ask, "What spirit is at work?" We also learned in chapter 3 that evangelism is central to Jesus' purpose in giving the Holy Spirit. Now, it is my observation that in many of the groups (and meetings) that make some of the greatest claims to spiritual power and manifestations there are very few people getting saved. This should make us ask why.

The focus in Mystical Religion is quite different. Spiritual experiences are to awaken us to our inner potential and individual importance. Prophecy tends to focus on our tremendous giftedness and personal destiny. A spirit of flattery tends to infuse personal "prophecies." Someone walks up to us and says, "Wow! You're so anointed, gifted, and filled with potential. I am surprised you haven't been given a greater position. Others may not see it, but I do. You have incredible things ahead." While it feels good, it's often flattery, which is spiritual and emotional manipulation designed to transfer our affection from others to them-selves. It's also, generally, a great way for the devil to get our eyes off of Jesus and onto ourselves and our "amazing gifts."

4. What Is the Role of Our Minds?

Biblical Religion teaches that our intellects are important

---

81 John 16:14

because God primarily reveals Himself through words.[82] Studying and memorizing Scripture is therefore important for every Christian, and the teaching of the Bible is central to public meetings. Our minds are important tools to help us discern things. In the same way, properly ordained church leaders are seen as important to bring discipline and growth in conformity to God's truth and ways.[83]

On the other hand, Mystical Religion teaches that the intellect is suspect because subjective, irrational experiences are foremost. People are often taught that the mind is an obstacle that keeps people from moving ahead. They are told not to let their mind rob them of receiving what God wants to do. The reason Satan wants us to get past our rational minds is because he wants to devalue the role of God's Word and the counsel of others. Then, he replaces them both with subjective feelings. The locus of authority moves from the objective to the subjective. As people fall deeper into these realms, they read the Bible less and less. Former pastors and teachers are abandoned and often become the object of jokes and derision because they are viewed as uninitiated skeptics who can't get past their supposed idolatry to the Bible.

While it is true that people can make an idol out of their intellect, and this is to be strenuously avoided, this does not mean that our intellect is to be abandoned. When we check our critical thinking at the door, we can get caught up into mere emotionalism, being drawn into foolish and unbiblical

---

[82] 1 Corinthians 2:12-13 "Now we have received, not the spirit of the world, but the Spirit who is from God, so that we may know the things freely given to us by God, which things we also speak, not in words taught by human wisdom, but in those taught by the Spirit, combining spiritual thoughts with spiritual words."
[83] Hebrews 13:17

practices. The Bible doesn't tell us to disengage our minds but rather to renew our minds.[84]

While it is understandable to trust people who seem to know more than we do and are portrayed as spiritual leaders, we must still measure what they say and do against the Bible's teaching. It is easy in our enthusiasm and hunger for God to simply get caught up in what is happening, but we must always practice discernment. Using our minds in conjunction with God's Word is honoring to the Holy Spirit. Then, we can find what is true and good and hold fast to it, rejoicing in confidence.

How do I Grow in Discernment?

First, study the Bible, memorize it, and learn what it says. Discernment is not primarily an inward feeling or impression. (Imagine trying to discern one inward impression by a second inward impression—which would you accept?) Discernment is much more than a subjective feeling. Think about it, if you find yourself lost in a forest, you don't determine the way out simply by how you feel. You need a compass. Our compass is the Word of God.

Discernment is a skill that comes from not only knowing God's Word but also knowing God Himself through a history of obeying Him. Hebrews 5:14 says, *"But solid food is for the mature, who because of practice have their senses trained to discern good and evil."* As you walk with God you gradually learn His ways. In so doing you become more experienced in recognizing what is truly of Him. This is why it is so important to be willing to listen to more experienced Christians. Remember, God tells us to test the

---

84 Romans 12:2

spirits, and you honor God when you do so in humility. If it's from God, it will stand up to the test.

Discernment also comes through being in submitted relationship to others in a healthy Christian community. God's plan is for our mutual dependence and submission. We are to function as parts of a whole and not be isolated. My friend Charles Simpson likes to point out the truth that "healthy things integrate and unhealthy things isolate."[85] A healthy animal will integrate into a herd, but a sick animal will isolate from the herd. A healthy family integrates into a larger community, but a dysfunctional family isolates, hiding many unhealthy habits and secrets.

The same is true on a spiritual level. Make sure that you integrate into a recognized, healthy church where you are in relationship with some of its leaders. Be very wary of those who want to be seen as spiritual leaders but are not in meaningful submission to a recognized local church. If you reverence God above any other desire, know and submit to the Bible, and listen to church leadership, then you do not have to fear being deceived.[86]

---

[85] Charles Simpson is an internationally known author, Bible teacher, and leader of leaders. His impact on the modern Church has been significant.

[86] Remember that submission is only proven when you are not in total agreement with a decision made by your church's leaders. If you are in full agreement with every decision, then there is nothing to submit to. Too many of God's people change churches when the first decision is made that they don't understand. They leave without approaching the leaders for understanding. This shows that they think they have already arrived and have nothing to learn. By submitting to leaders, you open yourself up to God teaching and developing you. If, after a time, your conscience will not allow you to stay, only then is it time to leave.

Chapter 7

The Importance of the Church

God, after He spoke long ago to the fathers in the prophets in many portions and in many ways, in these last days has spoken to us in His Son. - Hebrews 1:1-2

The Divine Shift

Under the Old Covenant in the Old Testament, God's primary way of speaking to His people was through prophets.[87] But Hebrews 1 signals a change. Now He speaks to us through His Son. The focus has shifted from the lone prophet to the Holy Spirit operating in the Church, which is Christ's multi-gifted Body.[88] Although Jesus physically ascended to heaven, He still has a Body on earth through which He speaks and ministers.

John the Baptist was a transitional figure, the last of the Old Testament prophets. He closed out the old

---

[87] This was because until the Day of Pentecost, the Holy Spirit had not yet been poured out upon all of God's people. The OT prophet was a temporary guardian over God's people in the same way that the Law was our temporary guardian - see Galatians 3:23-25; 4:1-3.

[88] Ephesians 1:22-23

order and introduced Jesus Christ as the head of a new order.[89] While some may wish we still had Old Testament prophets (or maybe even think of themselves as one), it was never God's intent that the Old Testament prophets continue. He had a better plan from the beginning. The great prophet Moses foreshadowed God's plan when he said, *"Would that all the Lord's people were prophets, that the Lord would put His Spirit upon them!"*[90] Moses' prayer was that all God's people would be able to hear His voice. This was God's continual promise throughout the Old Testament.[91]

The Old Testament prophet was a necessary but temporary office until the coming of Jesus Christ. The Old Covenant believer was not yet able to hear God's voice because the Holy Spirit had not yet been given.[92] But now that He has come, each of us can hear His voice and be led by Him.[93] The New Testament Church is God's plan to bring His people to maturity. A New Testament prophet, unlike the Old Testament prophet, is no longer God's voice to the world. The Holy Spirit operating through the multi-gifted Church is now His voice. A New Testament prophet takes his place with the four other spiritual offices Jesus has given to the Church to help it come to maturity.

So Christ Himself gave the apostles, the prophets, the evangelists, the pastors and teachers, to equip his people for works of service, so that the Body of Christ may be built up until we all reach unity in the faith and in the knowledge of

---

[89] Matthew 11:11-14
[90] Numbers 11:29
[91] Jeremiah 31:33-34; Isaiah 30:20-21; Joel 2:28. These OT scriptures were fulfilled in NT Acts 2:17-21 and 1 John 2:27.
[92] John 7:38-39
[93] John 10:27; Romans 8:14

the Son of God and become mature, attaining to the whole measure of the fullness of Christ.
- Ephesians 4:11-13, NIV

Notice that the fivefold ministers serve the Body so that it will be able to do the ministry, or "works of service." The focus is always on the whole Body. We no longer depend on spiritual superheroes. The Body of Christ has become the superhero!

The Riches of Christ's Body

A healthy, functioning church is a powerful storehouse of the riches of Christ with an ample supply for everyone. Our calling is to be used in our gifting to build up the Body until it displays the "fullness of Christ." God's plan is for our mutual dependence and submission to each other. We are to function as a whole and not be isolated from one another. In this way we all can come to maturity.

As a result, we are no longer to be children, tossed here and there by waves and carried about by every wind of doctrine, by the trickery of men, by craftiness in deceitful scheming; but speaking the truth in love, we are to grow up in all aspects into Him who is the head, even Christ, from whom the whole body, being fitted and held together by what every joint supplies, according to the proper working of each individual part, causes the growth of the body for the building up of itself in love.   - Ephesians 4:14-16

Notice that we are warned against the trickery and deceitful scheming of those who would bring divisions. Instead, we are to speak truth to each other to maintain our unity. We are to grow up into Christ as each member (or *"joint"*) properly works and brings in their needed supply to richly equip the whole Body.

Notice that the emphasis is on building up the whole Body. We are to seek the mutual good and not our own, individual, selfish ambition. The current overemphasis we hear in so much preaching today that focuses on "your destiny," "your dreams," and "your prosperity" is un-balanced at best. This emphasis on radical individualism is a result of our culture's influence, not the Bible's teaching. Individualism can be defined as putting the interests of the individual above everything else. It means that I seek my happiness, my glory, my destiny, and my fulfilment fore-most. But if I do that, I eventually end up spiritually impoverished, frustrated, and empty. This is because the fullness of Christ and His power and riches are not given to us individually but corporately.

An Army of One?

On January 1, 2001 the Army adopted a new recruiting campaign slogan meant to attract young people who were becoming increasingly self-focused. They chose the slogan "Army of One"—as if an army could be successful as a collection of individuals seeking personal self-fulfillment. An army's strength comes from individuals becoming joined into a united force.[94] The ad campaign predictably was a flop, and within four years the Army had missed its

---

[94] Loren Thompson, a defense analyst, once said, "If you want to be an 'Army of One' you probably want to join the Hell's Angels, not the U.S. Army." (see "'Army Strong' Replaces ' Army of One'" by the Associated Press on NBCNews.com.(http://www.nbcnews.com/id/15197720/ns/us_news-military /t/army-strong-replaces-army-one/#.XdXXcVdKhPY)

recruiting target by the widest margin in more than two decades. Compare this to the continuing success of the Marine Corps recruiting, which has had the same slogan for many decades: "The Few. The Proud. The Marines." This speaks to the desire in all of us to accomplish something great by striving to become a part of something much greater than ourselves.

God's mystery of the Church is revealed in this: As I truly serve and live in fellowship with the Body, I become enriched. Unfortunately, much of today's teaching and worship songs are focused on radical individualism. Just listen to how often the words "me" and "I," as opposed to "we" and "us," occur in most popular worship songs today. Instead of fully experiencing the power of being the Body of Christ gathered together, we sing songs mostly about "my feelings" and hear sermons about "my prosperity" and "my destiny."[95] In order to experience the fullness of Christ's riches, we must understand the importance of the Church and how the Holy Spirit works through it.

Keeping the Right Balance

An important way that the Holy Spirit works to build the Church is through spiritual gifts. When it comes to spiritual gifts and manifestations, there are really only three paths to take—and only one of them is right. On either side of the

---

[95] Why go to church to have an individualized experience and hear a message aimed at your personal happiness? You can do this at home by listening to a podcast. And people are getting the message—"It's all about me"—so the average Christian stays home more and more on Sundays. They have lost sight of the riches and power of the fellowship of the Body.

balanced, prudent approach that the Bible teaches is an unhelpful extreme that we are warned against.

> *Do not quench the Spirit; do not despise prophetic utterances. But examine everything carefully; hold fast to that which is good.   - 1 Thessalonians 5:19-21*

It's easy and tempting to fall into one of the incorrect extremes that the above verse warns us against. Rather than staying in the middle of the path, many Christians and churches fall into one of the ditches on either side:

Mistake #1: To despise prophecy and other manifestation gifts and thereby quench the Spirit.

Because of problems, confusion, and past experiences where people have been deceived, some despise prophecy and spiritual gifts by saying, "We can do without them." It's a temptation to feel this way in reaction to much of the spiritual foolishness we encounter. The problem, however, is that when you embrace this mentality, you are shutting out much of the influence of the third Person of the Trinity! The above scripture warns us not to despise prophetic utterances—God sends them for our edification, for encouragement, for guidance in His work, and for building up His Church. We need to listen to the voice of the Holy Spirit. Do not let the chaff of false or empty, carnal prophecies sour you so that you miss the kernels of true prophesy that God does give. We need to let the chaff blow away in the wind and hold onto the true.

It is a form of pride to ignore our need for prophecy and spiritual gifts. It is making the claim that we can live the Christian life and build His kingdom by our own under- standing and ability. We can't limit ourselves to what we can control and explain fully. 1 Corinthians 14:1 tells us to "desire earnestly spiritual gifts but especially that you may prophesy." Forsaking them is a mistake that will leave our ministries and lives without the needed, overcoming power that God has appropriated for us.

Mistake #2: To be gullible and foolish

The opposite error is just as bad. Some people are so zealous for the supernatural that they don't exercise dis- cernment and common sense. The above verse tells us to examine everything carefully and only hold onto the good and true. Not every seemingly supernatural manifestation or supposed prophecy is from the Lord.

Some people are so desperate to hear from God that they accept whatever thoughts pop into their heads when praying–even when these thoughts or impressions are directly contrary to what the Bible teaches. Think about it: if the Holy Spirit inspired the scriptures, and the scriptures say God doesn't change, why would the Holy Spirit tell you to do something the Bible has forbidden? As a pastor I have had people tell me things like: "God told me it was okay to leave my husband and children because the Holy Spirit has shown me that I made a mistake and that this new man really was God's choice to be my husband." The truth is that the Holy Spirit will never diminish the importance of Scripture but will always draw us back to what He has said once for all in the scriptures.

It has been said that "God speaks to us half as often as we think, but when He does, He means it twice as seriously as we take it." When God speaks to us, He means it to be taken seriously and obeyed. I have found that God usually waits for me to do what He last told me before He says something fresh to me. I have also found that whenever He has truly spoken to me, it has always been significant, and when I have obeyed, it has always produced great and lasting fruit. This is one test of whether something was really of the Lord: Does it produce a significant and lasting effect?[96] God will never speak so often that His voice becomes a common thing that we take lightly and then forget what He has said. This is most often just our imagination at work.)

The Importance of Right Motivation

In order to lay hold of Christ's riches, we must examine our motivation. The truth of the matter is, as fallen humanity, it's tempting to seek fulfillment of our own desires over pursuing obedience to God. Wrong motives are and can be

---

[96] Isaiah 55:10-11 "For as the rain and the snow come down from heaven, and do not return there without watering the earth and making it bear and sprout, and furnishing seed to the sower and bread to the eater; so will My word be which goes forth from My mouth; It will not return to Me empty, without accomplishing what I desire, and without succeeding in the matter for which I sent it."
Jeremiah 23:28-30 "'The prophet who has a dream may relate his dream, but let him who has My word speak My word in truth. What does straw have in common with grain?' declares the LORD. 'Is not My word like fire?' declares the LORD, 'and like a hammer which shatters a rock? Therefore behold, I am against the prophets,' declares the LORD, 'who steal My words from each other.'"

a real impediment to walking in the truth. We are warned about this in Paul's second letter to Timothy:

For the time will come when they will not endure sound doctrine; but wanting to have their ears tickled, they will accumulate for themselves teachers in accordance with their own desires, and will turn away their ears from the truth and will turn aside to myths. - 2 Timothy 4:3-4

Paul points out the danger of being motivated by wrong desires and agendas. It can lead us astray. We get a powerful example of this from the life of Jesus in John 6. Jesus fed a very hungry crowd of 5,000 people by multiplying five loaves and two fish. Everyone ate to the full, and there was still food left over. Their full stomachs felt good (full stomachs weren't common in the ancient world). This made Jesus very popular. Later, during the night, Jesus and His disciples left that location. When the people woke up in the morning they discovered that Jesus was gone.

So when the crowd saw that Jesus was not there, nor His disciples, they themselves got into the small boats, and came to Capernaum seeking Jesus. When they found Him on the other side of the sea, they said to Him, "Rabbi, when did You get here?" Jesus answered them and said, "Truly, truly, I say to you, you seek Me, not because you saw signs, but because you ate of the loaves and were filled." - John 6:24-26

Now, it's kind of puzzling when you first read this passage. Why did Jesus rebuke them? After all, the people got up and went searching for Jesus. Isn't that a good thing? And yet Jesus rebuked them. He knew that they followed Him not because the signs convinced them that He was God, but because they wanted some more food for free. Jesus knows that people can seek Him for the wrong reason.

People can seek religion, go to church, and search out spiritual manifestations for the wrong reasons. They can just be seeking some perceived personal benefit. They may just want the spectacle, the emotional high, the temporary escape, the status, money, reputation, visibility, or whatever it may be. Jesus implies that they ought to have sought Him out "because you saw signs."

Now, here's the interesting thing about signs: They point beyond themselves.

The Purpose of Signs and Wonders

If you see an arrow-shaped sign that says, "This way to the zoo," and you stand there and stare at the sign all day, you've missed the point. You are not going to see any animals. It is completely foolish to become focused on or obsessed with a sign. You have to go where the sign is pointing.

When Jesus took the five loaves and two fishes and fed 5,000 people, it was a sign that God was present. There was far more being offered to them than a full stomach, but they became focused on the sign itself because their motive was for some immediate, earthly benefit, even more than their desire for God.

In some meetings, I have witnessed the focus set on seeing signs and wonders. All the excitement is on trying to see angels, angel feathers, gold dust, orbs, gems, unusual smells, certain feelings, or dramatic physical manifestations. If people believe that these things were present, then it was a good meeting. If not, then the meeting was a disappointment. When being obsessed with signs becomes our driving motivation, it can lead to deception. It opens the door to wish fulfilment, psychological manipulation or trickery by unscrupulous ministers, and even demonic activity. Whenever people get obsessed with the signs, it means they have taken their eye off the true goal which is Jesus, becoming like Him, and leading others to Him. The signs have become idols.

Later in John 6, after refusing to provide the people with any more physical bread, Jesus tells them that the bread they ate, and were again seeking, was just a sign that He was the true bread.[97] He tells them that they must likewise absorb Him into themselves and exchange their life for His.[98] But the crowds were unwilling to accept this and abandoned Him.

On hearing it, many of His disciples said, "This is a hard teaching. Who can accept it?" ...From this time many of His disciples turned back and no longer followed Him.
- John 6:60, 66, NIV

The problem with these that turned away is that they had only come to Him to see signs.[99] Only those who recognized that Jesus' challenging teaching could lead them to eternal life continued on with Him.[100] Even today

---

[97] John 6:35 "Jesus said to them, 'I am the bread of life; he who comes to Me will not hunger, and he who believes in Me will never thirst.'"

[98] John 6:51, 56 "I am the living bread that came down out of heaven; if anyone eats of this bread, he will live forever; and the bread also which I will give for the life of the world is My flesh...He who eats My flesh and drinks My blood abides in Me, and I in him."

[99] John 6:2

[100] John 6:67-69

many people are attracted to aspects of Jesus and Christianity but draw back from God's full remedy for their need. They don't like to hear that they are prone to sin and that the remedy requires repentance and a full surrender to Christ. Jesus tells us to take up our cross[101], which means dying to ourselves and our selfish desires. Nothing else will bring spiritual maturity into a person's life—not even going to Bible college, writing a big check to the church, or having a multitude of dreams and visions.

The Cross Is Uppermost

The apostle Paul's life was a demonstration of this. Paul saw many miracles, signs, and wonders through his ministry. He healed many people and had many accomplishments, but he only gloried in the power of the cross.

> *But may it never be that I would boast, except in the cross of our Lord Jesus Christ through which the world has been crucified to me, and I to the world.* - *Galatians 6:14*[102]

Paul warned Timothy of false teachers who taught a type of Christianity that had the *"form of godliness, although they have denied its power."*[103] They taught a form of Christianity where the cross was not the central focus for their followers. A modern expression of this is what I call "pop religion." Like pop art, it's popular but is not truly valuable and will not endure. It uses the same language as true Christianity but lacks its power because it focuses only on God's love and affirmation and treats Christianity as a

---

[101] Luke 9:23
[102] See also Galatians 2:20
[103] 2 Timothy 3:5

means to self-fulfillment. It focuses on fantastic experiences and feelings while neglecting our call to take up our cross and follow Jesus. But the Bible tells us that the cross is the power of Christianity.[104] This was the true power that the false teachers denied. Only a cross-centered Christianity truly changes lives. Pop religion is just an empty distraction. **The truest demonstration of God's power is not a body that shakes or a bank account that grows but rather a life that is transformed into the image of Christ.**

The Importance of Oversight

The idea that "The more out of control you are, the more in control the Spirit is," is not a Christian idea but a pagan one. God is not a God of disorder; He is a God of order.

> *For God is not a God of confusion but of peace, as in all the churches of the saints. - 1 Corinthians 14:33*

The Holy Spirit does not require an atmosphere of chaos in order to work. He doesn't need people shouting, running around the room, and dancing wildly to move among us. When we create these sorts of wild scenes, we actually hinder the work of the Holy Spirit and encourage people to act carnally and, often, nonsensically.

On the other hand, the Holy Spirit is aided when we practice discernment and don't let things which are not of Him take control of a meeting. The presence of mere emotionalism or spurious activity is never helpful to the work of the Spirit. Wise pastoral oversight is a necessary aid to the Holy Spirit's work.

---

[104] Romans 1:16; 1 Corinthians 1:18

Years ago, I feared offending the Holy Spirit by possibly making a mistake in correcting anyone's behavior in a meeting. As a result, we suffered through many distracting, carnal displays. My reticence probably came from unhelpful teaching I had received. Because the Holy Spirit was symbolized as a dove at Jesus' baptism, some get the notion that the Spirit is skittish like a bird (but remember that on the Day of Pentecost He was symbolized as fire). There is the belief among some that if we make one wrong move, the Holy Spirit will become offended and flit off like birds on a telephone wire who hear a loud noise.

But the Holy Spirit is not a bird, He is the third person of the Godhead. And we know that God is not easily offended and flighty but is rather long suffering, gracious, and patient with us. The Holy Spirit is not thin skinned. He has the same character and personality as the Father and the Son.

We are told, "Do not grieve the Holy Spirit of God," but that is given in the context of teaching about angry words, gossip, unwholesome speech, and slander, not pastoral correction of excessive behavior.[105] We are also told not to "quench the Spirit," but then in the next two verses we are told to "examine everything carefully" and to only "hold fast to that which is good."[106] Clearly, we are not told that the Holy Spirit requires a hands-off, anything-goes, free-for-all environment in order to work. If God didn't want any correction when spiritual manifestations are present, why did He give us directions on how to do just that in 1 Corinthians 14?

Some teach that in order to have true spiritual

---

[105] Ephesians 4:29-31
[106] 1 Thessalonians 5:19-22

manifestations, we must allow fake manifestations to take place alongside them. A very well-known charismatic leader once said:

"I've seen a lot of fake, but I've seen a lot of real. The real's worth it. I will allow the fake. I don't want the fake on the platform, because I don't want to promote the fake, but I'll allow the fake in the room because I so believe in the genuine. I've had people say over the years that, 'Some of this seems fake.'

I go, 'It is!'

They go, 'What?'

I go, 'Most of it's fake.'

They go, 'What do you mean?'

I say, 'I've watched this for 40 years. Most places that I've been, the majority of the manifestations are not caused by the Holy Spirit.'

They go, 'Really?'

But I said, 'The problem is it's not all fake. And the genuine is in our midst. And I will allow a whole lot of Hamburger Helper to allow the genuine to take place.' I said, 'I won't promote it, but I will allow it.'"[107]

In that same video he says that 80% of the manifestations in his meetings are fake, that they are not genuine

---

[107] "The Word Like Fire: A Mike Bickle explanation for allowing fake manifestations of the Holy Spirit" https://thewordlikefire.wordpress.com/2019/04/28/a-mike-bickle-explanation-for-allowing-fake-manifestations-of-the-holy-spirit/ Watch imbedded video beginning at the 5:30 mark to 6:15 or look up the original video online: "Manifestations of the Spirit: Real or Fake? Mike Bickle's Perspective Part 1 https://www.youtube.com/watch?v=wZtFg4J7rkk&t=393s

manifestations of the Holy Spirit. I do not understand why some people believe that we must just allow the fake in order to see any genuine manifestations of the Holy Spirit. Does it really honor the Holy Spirit to allow the fake? Isn't it possible that the Holy Spirit could be offended when fake manifestations are identified as His work and celebrated in His name?

The truth is that the greatest impediment to people accepting prophecy and the gifts of the Spirit are not those who teach that such gifts are no longer for today but rather those who carelessly misrepresent the Holy Spirit and bring the Spirit's work into disrepute by their actions and claims. We ought to be cautious of attaching God's name to things that might not be from Him.

It is certainly possible to be so heavy-handed in leading a meeting that people become afraid of making a mistake and being publicly corrected. If we do so, people will shut down out of fear of embarrassment. This must, of course, be carefully avoided. But don't you think there is a healthy balance where the Holy Spirit and individuals who are learning can both be honored? This can happen if we teach our people properly and any necessary correction is done privately in an encouraging manner. If oversight is done humbly, cautiously, and graciously, we need not fear that the Holy Spirit will become offended and flit off.

The Church, not the isolated individual, is the focal point of the Holy Spirit's work to advance the kingdom of God. In the next chapter we will look at how the Holy Spirit brings God's kingdom into our circumstances.

Chapter 8

The Kingdom Breaks In

Which of the following is correct to say? "I have been saved," "I am being saved," or "one day I shall be saved"? If you chose all three, then congratulations, you are correct.

The Bible teaches that:

- **We have been saved.**[108]

- **We are being saved**[109]

- **We shall be saved**[110]

We have been completely saved from sin's guilt, are progressively being saved from sin's power,[111] and we look forward to the day when, in heaven, sin will hold no attraction to us. In the meantime, we stand upon the gift of eternal salvation won for us by Christ, try to grow in our

---

[108] 2 Timothy 1:9; John 3:36; John 5:24
[109] 1 Corinthians 1:18; 2 Corinthians 2:15; Philippians 1:6
[110] Romans 5:9-10; Romans 13:11; Matthew 25:46
[111] That is, we have greater victory in some areas and yet continue to struggle in others, all the while striving for further victory.

present experience of that salvation,[112] and look forward to its final fulfilment in the next life.

So much of our confusion and struggle as Christians comes from the reality of having been established in our salvation but not yet experiencing it in its fullness. We wonder just how much of our inheritance we can experience now. The great majority of us reject the claim made by a few that they have already achieved sinless perfection. Probably none of us would accept someone saying that they will never be injured, have sorrow, get sick, or die (as will be true in heaven). But how much of our future inheritance can we expect to have now?

Already but Not Yet

The kingdom of God is the realm in which Jesus' will is being done and His works accomplished. It is where people are being reconciled to God and each other, demons are being cast out, and sick people are healed. It is the dominion where Jesus is worshiped and followed as King.

In regard to this kingdom, theologians talk about the mystery of the **"already but not yet" dynamic.** Jesus has **already** inaugurated a new expansion of the kingdom of God in His first coming but has **not yet** brought its full, ultimate expression. That awaits His second coming. Jesus taught, *"The time is fulfilled, and the kingdom of God is at hand,"*[113] that *"the kingdom of God is in your midst,"*[114] and that people could *"enter the kingdom."*[115]

On the other hand, Jesus taught us to pray for the

---

112 Philippians 2:12b-13
113 Mark 1:15
114 Luke 17:21
115 John 3:5; Luke 18:24; Matthew 11:12

future coming of the kingdom to rule on earth as it does in heaven,[116] and said on the last night of His life that He would *"not drink of the fruit of the vine from now on until the kingdom of God comes."*[117]

What are we to make of Jesus' teaching? It is this: Jesus has *already* brought the kingdom but has *not yet* brought it in its fullness. We are *already* experiencing life in this kingdom now but are *not yet* experiencing that life in its fullness. That will not happen until He brings the fullness of the kingdom with His second coming. The kingdom is more fully present than in the times of the Old Testament saints but not as fully present as when Christ returns. Only then will we know total victory.

All of this presents us with an enigma. The key is to find the right biblical balance. It is easy to lag behind and fail to lay hold of the measure of the kingdom we have been given. Certainly, it is undeniable that many churches and Christians fall far short of exercising their full kingdom authority. Jesus wants us to press into His promises and His anointing. It is encouraging to see there is now much more interest in such subjects as the kingdom of God and spiritual gifts.

On the other hand, it is also easy to run ahead and claim a fuller measure of the kingdom than we have been given. When we do this, we claim for ourselves greater powers than what we legitimately have. Paul had firsthand experience with mystical Christians who were making exaggerated boasts of their spiritual abilities, authority, and accomplishments. In their minds they had outstripped Paul and his associates who had brought the gospel to Corinth.

---

[116] Matthew 6:10
[117] Luke 22:18

You are already filled, you have already become rich, you have become kings without us; and indeed, I wish that you had become kings so that we also might reign with you.
- 1 Corinthians 4:8

These believers were claiming to already be filled and complete. As we have seen, the truth is that we already enjoy some of the riches Christ has won for us, but we must wait until we die or Christ returns to have it all. These "super saints" in Corinth claimed to already have it all. They thought of themselves as spiritually full and reigning on the earth. Paul points out that their claims were premature. When the time for the fullness of our reign in Christ comes, then Paul will reign with them (and us). This is the meaning of the last phrase of the verse. Their claims were premature, exaggerated, and delusional. Paul goes on to contrast their claims of being super-spiritual kings with his experience as a true apostle, which included weakness, dishonor, hunger, hard work, suffering, etc.[118]

Paul had lovingly admonished them to "*...learn not to exceed what is written, so that no one of you will become arrogant in behalf of one against the other.*"[119] Paul told them that if they would let the Old Testament scriptures and the apostolic writings (later to become the New Testament) be their guide, they would not go into spiritual deception and factions.

Fooling Ourselves

An inflated sense of our spirituality makes it difficult to

---

[118] 1 Corinthians 4:9-14
[119] 1 Corinthians 4:6

discern the source of inner impressions. For instance, we can have dreams and visions that are truly God-given but also dreams and visons that are simply from our own imaginations. Paul warned us of allowing these works of imagination to distract us from focusing on the reality of Christ, which is our prize.

> *Let no one keep defrauding you of your prize by delighting in self-abasement and the worship of the angels, taking his stand on visions he has seen, inflated without cause by his fleshly mind, and not holding fast to the head [which is Christ].*
> *- Colossians 2:18-19a*

Paul alerts us to the danger of becoming puffed up and led astray by visions and dreams that are merely from the human imagination or fleshly mind. Not every dream, mental image, or thought that pops up is from the Holy Spirit. In a hyped-up environment where we are taught unrealistic expectations of our spiritual capacities, it is easy for people to confuse the merely human and natural for divine communication. Failure to discern the difference gradually increases our vulnerability to actual demonic deception.[120] It is essential that we gain a right understanding of this "already but not yet" paradigm. One area where many of us struggle with this is divine healing.

Divine Healing

Since God our Creator has given our bodies mechanisms that allow us to restore tissue, create anti-bodies, and

---

[120] Notice that the above verse also mentions an unhealthy interest in angels, which is also a hallmark contemporary mystical Christianity.

replenish cells, we can say that all healing is from God. However, when we speak of divine healing or the gift of healing, we are talking about healing that comes from the direct action or intervention of God.

Healings can range from simple cases like a cold or headache to very remarkable ones that draw widespread attention.

A longtime member of our church, Jimmy Craig, had a remarkable healing. He injured his back in an industrial accident and had to have surgery. During the surgery, a scalpel cut through most of his spinal cord. The surgeon closed him up, and a blood clot formed to crush what was left of his spinal cord. Jim awoke in the hospital to discover that he had no feeling or control below his waist. He had no use of his legs and was diagnosed to be 100% disabled. He spent the next three years in a wheelchair with the prognosis of being confined to it for the rest of his life. One night, his son brought him to a meeting at our church. Marc Dupont, founder of Mantle of Praise ministries, was leading the meeting.

Marc had the pastoral staff gather around Jim, lay hands on him, and join Marc in prayer. At first, Jimmy didn't feel anything, but after a few minutes he felt strength and feeling returning to his legs. He turned to his son and said, "I feel like I could stand up." He stood up without assistance, and though his legs were atrophied from three years in a wheelchair, he felt steady on his feet. "I think I can walk," he said, and he began to walk across the entire church auditorium twice. Of course, by now he had drawn people's attention, and there was rejoicing in the church. He went home afterwards and surprised his wife and daughter. They went for a long walk in the neighborhood till midnight, praising the Lord.

When he went to see his specialist doctors, they had no explanation other than that a miracle had taken place. In the years since, Jim has had total use of his legs and has led an active, full life. His story has been recorded in several books, on television shows, and he has told his testimony live to thousands.

It is obvious to even a casual reader of the New Testament that healing played a big part in the founding of Jesus' Church and in His ministry. He sent His disciples out on missions to preach the gospel and heal the sick, and He healed the sick Himself. After Jesus ascended, the early Church grew in an atmosphere of powerful healings. Today, the ministry of healing still needs to have an important place in the Church.

However, the subject of healing is one that is filled with much controversy and confusion. We wonder why some people are healed while many others are not. Sometimes those who seem the most deserving, who have been the most faithful Christians, or who have the most people depending upon them (a young father or mother for instance) are not healed, while someone we may deem less deserving is. We keep hoping to crack the code and find the formula that will guarantee healing. Many people have written books claiming that they know the key to healing, but has anyone really discovered a key? Has anyone found the secret to being healed?

The Place of Faith in Healing

On a number of occasions Jesus specifically associated a person's healing with faith.[121] So we say, "That must be the

---

[121] Matthew 9:22; Mark 10:52; etc.

key! If I just have faith, I will be healed." A problem with this view is that in the great majority of healings, Jesus did not make reference to the person's faith.[122] Jesus healed when a man confessed to having weak faith.[123] Some were even healed who seemed to have little or no faith.[124] If you read the scriptures in the footnotes below, you will see that this idea—that it is the strength of our faith that brings healing—has many scriptural problems.

Another problem with this teaching is that it leads to blaming the victim. When someone isn't healed, some will say it's because they didn't have enough faith, or there must be some sin in their life that is blocking the healing, or maybe it's some mysterious family curse, etc. While it's true that unforgiveness or a lack of repentance may be factors in some instances, they do not explain the great majority of cases where people were not healed.

Finally, this view doesn't fit with what we see. We have seen people with little faith healed, and those with seemingly great faith not healed. I imagine that this has been your experience as well. I have talked to many ministers that have very significant healing ministries and they confess that it remains a mystery to them as well.

After many years I have come to this conclusion regarding faith and healing: If you believe that God heals people and you are willing to ask Him to heal you, then you have sufficient faith. If you are not healed, you shouldn't just assume that you have done something wrong or that your faith was insufficient. And it certainly wasn't because you didn't use the right formula in your prayers, nor was it

---

[122] Luke 7:11-14; Matthew 14:14; John 11:38-44; etc.
[123] Mark 9:24; see also Matthew 14:28-31 when Peter fails while walking on water.
[124] Luke 22:48-51; John 11:43-44; John 5:5-9; Luke 8:26-39

because you allowed negative thoughts to slip into your mind.[125] One thing I feel certain about: healing should not be seen as a payment to those who can work up a sufficient level of faith or get some formula just right.

It is vital, however, that we remember the importance of faith in the ministry of healing. Remember, in the New Testament we found that faith is mentioned in connection with healing. There are therefore, I believe, two mistakes we must avoid. One is to believe that a sufficient level of faith will always guarantee healing. The other is to assume that since faith can't guarantee healing, it must not be that important. This will lead us to become complacent in the area of healing. The simple fact is that the more faith we have in regard to healing, the more healings we will see.

You see, where there is little faith for healing, few people will pray for it and so few, if any, will be healed. Where there is more faith, you will have more prayer and you will see more healings. But where there is much faith, you will see much prayer and even more and greater healings. People with faith actively pray for the sick and will pray with perseverance.

When my son, Neil, who is one of our pastors, was in his late 20s, he injured his back while wakeboarding. X-rays revealed a badly herniated disk. For the next four years he experienced frequent pain, had to be careful of his activity, and was unable to hold any of his children for any lengthy period of time. Over the course of four years, people prayed for his healing many times.

One evening at a healing meeting, there was a word of knowledge that God was going to heal backs. Neil went

---

[125] Some of the teachings regarding healing have more in common with Religious Science's "mind over matter" doctrine than with biblical teaching.

forward once again to get prayer. As he stood there waiting and worshipping, he sensed the Lord ask him, "Would you like Me to heal you tonight?" Another one of our pastors, Mike Cook, who also suffered from back pain and had also received prayer a number of times without any relief, did not go forward but remained in his seat worshipping. While he was worshipping, he felt God's healing power come on his back and all the pain disappeared. He was permanently healed! Filled with excitement and faith, he quickly went forward to pray for others. He saw my son standing there waiting and said, "God just healed my back, and I am filled with faith to pray for someone else's healing." As he prayed, Neil was instantly healed. Neil wanted to testify of his healing to the unsaved chiropractor who had been treating him. He told the chiropractor of his healing and requested that new x-rays be taken. The x-rays showed clearly that the bulging disk had been completely restored.

This demonstrates that churches that regularly and persistently pray for healing will see healings. Both of these two men sought prayer a number of times before they were healed. It is also worth noting that one went forward for prayer that night and the other didn't, but both were healed. This story also demonstrates that sometimes healings come in clusters, and God's healing power is present at some times more than others. It also shows how words of knowledge are often used in healing. Finally, there were others present that night who were not healed. And so we come around again to the mystery regarding healing.

Healing and the Kingdom

Healing is an expression of the kingdom. Healing takes place today because the kingdom has **already** partially come; however, others are not healed because the kingdom has **not yet** fully come. Why the kingdom breaks in to heal in some cases and not in others is known to God alone. I heard John Wimber say once that some prayers for healing are answered with "not yet" rather than "now."[126] One thing we know for sure is that everyone will be healed when they get to heaven and enter the fullness of the kingdom.

Another important reason to actively pray for the sick is that prayer always brings benefit. Prayer brings God's grace, for God is always faithful to hear our prayers. It is not the case that healing is the only benefit that our prayers can bring. Often, our prayers for the healing of the sick bring peace, relief from suffering, deliverance from fear, and God's comfort to the afflicted one and their loved ones. They can even be used to bring someone to salvation.

One day, our office received a call to go pray for a man who lay in a hospital in a coma, with little hope for survival. This man was unknown to anyone in our office. One of our pastors, Jim Deyling, stopped by to pray for him. When he arrived, the man was unconscious and alone in his room. As Jim began praying, a powerful sense of the Lord filled the room. There was no change in the man, but the next day Jim returned to pray for him again because of the strong sense of the Lord's presence from the previous day. Once again as he prayed, a mighty sense of the Lord filled the room, and Jim expected that the man would make a full recovery although he was still in a coma. When he returned on the third day, the man was awake but he could not speak because of the tubes in his throat. Sensing that the man was not a Christian, Jim led him to the Lord, the man

---

[126] John Wimber was the longtime leader of the Vineyard Church movement until his death in 1997

responding with hand signals. After Jim led him in prayer, the man had huge tears running down his face. He had clearly met Jesus.

On the fourth day, Jim went to visit the man, but he was unconscious. This time his mother and girlfriend were there, and they told Jim the man's story. He was now 36, but when he was 12 he had started coming to our church through our outreach program called Youth Venture. He gave his life to the Lord and was baptized. Shortly after this, he moved out of state to live with his father, which was a terrible experience. The boy's life spiraled downhill. He got involved with drugs and alcohol, and when he got older he joined an outlaw motorcycle gang and ended up going to prison several times. He was in several relationships where he had been physically abusive. It was a tragic story to hear. Jim prayed for the man again before leaving, and the next day the man died. Jim's prayers had not healed the man but had brought him out of a coma so that he could be restored to Jesus and go to heaven when he died. He received the greatest healing possible. God is so full of mercy.

Rightly Understanding Our Kingdom Authority

"But Jesus has given us authority!" some will argue. "He won victory on the cross, so we have authority over sickness and death too." This is taught by some, but I believe it is a misunderstanding of Scripture.[127] We must

---

[127] I realize that I am getting into an area where many people have different views. I once held a different view than the one I have now, but I came to alter my view through years of Bible study and praying for the sick. We need to accept those whose sincere beliefs are different than ours, and we all need to be open to modify our opinions.

understand the great difference between healing and the forgiveness which brings eternal salvation.

Consider what the Bible teaches about sin and our guilt before God.

But you know that He appeared so that He might take away our sins. And in Him is no sin.   - 1 John 3:5, NIV

But He has appeared once for all at the culmination of the ages to do away with sin by the sacrifice of Himself.
- Hebrews 9:26, NIV

The above verses demonstrate that Christ has done away with the sins we have committed. The guilt that separated us from God is completely taken away. Therefore, if we pray the sinner's prayer with someone who is sincere, we can be 100% certain that their sins are forgiven and they are restored to God. In God's eyes they are sinless and can stand before Him now and for all eternity.

Likewise, the Bible teaches us that the devil and his demons have been completely conquered by Christ's work of the cross.

Therefore, since the children share in flesh and blood, He Himself likewise partook of the same, that through death He might render powerless him who had the power of death, that

is, the devil, and might free those who through fear of death were subject to slavery all their lives.   - Hebrews 2:14-15

Behold, I have given you authority to tread upon serpents and scorpions, and over all the power of the enemy, and nothing will injure you. Nevertheless do not rejoice in this, that the spirits are subject to you, but rejoice that your names are written in heaven. - Luke 10:19-20

Satan and his demons have been completely conquered! Therefore when we resist the devil, he will flee from us.[128] We can have total confidence that we can cast out every demon. Sin and demons are vanquished foes. We have total authority over them.

However, when it comes to our physical condition, we read something quite different. This enemy will not be finally overcome until the resurrection at the end of time.

For He must reign until He has put all His enemies under His feet. The last enemy that will be abolished is death. - 1 Corinthians 15:25-26

Death is the last enemy that Christ must put under His feet. Sickness and death are both a result of the frailness of our physical bodies which must be changed before we can inherit heaven. This same chapter tells us that *"flesh and blood cannot inherit the kingdom of God."*[129] Sickness and death are linked. Most people enter death through sickness. Only when physical death is defeated will sickness be finally defeated.

Think about it, our guilt from sin was a spiritual condition that Jesus spiritually paid for and removed.

---

[128] James 4:7
[129] 1 Corinthians 15:50

Likewise, demons are spiritual enemies whose power Jesus spiritually broke from over us.

But sickness and disease are in a different realm. They are physical conditions. They are in the physical and not the spiritual realm.[130] The physical realm will not be redeemed until Christ returns and God makes a new heaven and a new earth and we are physically changed.[131] Our newborn spirits are still wed to a physical body subject to corruption. Paul writes that *"we have this treasure in earthen vessels...but though our outer man is decaying, yet our inner man is being renewed day by day" (2 Corinthians 4:7, 16)*. We live in an imperfect, fallen world, where entropy and decay happen. Aging itself is a symptom of this, and not many people seriously pray for others to stop aging. Sickness is a part of death, and it will be around until our last enemy is put under Jesus' feet.

Can you see that there is a crucial difference between sin's guilt and demonic bondage on the one hand and healing on the other? Isn't this true in your experience? When you offer God's plan of forgiveness and salvation, you have complete confidence that the person you pray with will be saved if they sincerely meet the condition of repentance and faith. Likewise, you should have total confidence that the person will be delivered from demonic bondage and curses.[132] But do you honestly have that same confidence when you pray for a sick person?

---

[130] In some unusual cases, physical symptoms may have demonic causes; see Luke 13:11; Matthew 9:32-33; Mark 9:17-18. In these cases, since the physical condition is caused by the direct action of a demon, the person is set free from the condition when they are delivered from the demon.

[131] 2 Peter 3:13; Romans 8:20-23; 2 Corinthians 5:2-4; Philippians 3:20-21.

[132] This is assuming they have full understanding of Christ's victory and are willing to renounce and abandon the sin that gave the demon entrance.

Presumption Is Different from Faith

There is a great difference between faith and presumption. Faith involves claiming a divine promise that clearly applies to you. For instance, the Scripture says, *"For whoever will call upon the Lord will be saved."*[133] Clearly, this means that anyone who calls upon Jesus for salvation can claim this verse for themselves. Presumption, however, is different.

Presumption is the insistence on claiming something God has not specifically promised to me. It is often the result of selecting a particular verse, taken out of context, and insisting on a particular interpretation of that verse and applying it to fit my desire. Generally, the interpretation is not in alignment with the overall teaching of Scripture on the subject and it ignores conflicting scriptures. Usually that interpretation is also out of step with the experience of generations of God's people. When we accept teaching that doesn't hold up to careful scriptural scrutiny, we are in danger of spreading confusion.

For instance, I have been present a number of times when someone has "prophesied" over a dying person, "Thou shalt live and not die." I am sorry to report that in every case the person has gone on to die, and their loved ones, who had accepted those words spoken so confidently in the name of the Lord, were thrown into

---

[133] Romans 10:13

confusion and a faith crisis because the words failed.[134] Now, clearly those who made the pronouncement did not have a specific word that the person would recover. Much harm is done by people who act in a presumptuous manner based upon unsound teaching they have received regarding their supposed "authority as a believer."

Let me give you one more example. There is an unfortunate postscript to the story told earlier in the chapter regarding the man whom Pastor Jim prayed for in the hospital three times, who then subsequently died after being led to Christ. Unbeknownst to Jim, there was another couple who prayed for him in the hospital, who coincidently attended our church. They had told the man's mother that God would certainly heal her son. When he died, they assured her that God was going to do a greater work and raise him from the dead. They convinced her to not let his organs be taken by the doctors to be donated to others waiting for a transplant. When Jim learned of this, he contacted the people (since they were members of our church) and tried to gently help them understand how their views were faulty and their actions had not been helpful to the family. Instead of receiving this gentle correction, they accused Jim of not having faith and not understanding the power of the Holy Spirit.

---

[134] Apparently those who make such pronouncements do so on the basis of Psalm 118:17 where the psalmist (presumably King David) pronounced, "I shall not die but live, and tell of the works of the Lord." The psalm recounts that David was being pursued by enemies who sought his life. He evidently had a personal assurance from the Lord that they would not be successful. He would outlive their efforts and tell of the Lord's goodness. These words pertained to King David and are not a promise for all to claim. Whereas the words "Thou shalt live and not die" do not appear anywhere in Scripture, the words "Thou shall die and not live" (2 Kings 20:1) were pronounced by the prophet Isaiah to King Hezekiah. It is interesting to note that I have never heard those words pronounced over anyone.

Of course, the folly of their approach is obvious to all. The man did not recover or rise from the dead, and his organs that would have helped others, maybe even saving lives, were lost. Like many other fanatics today, the "prophesying" couple refused kind instruction, left the church, and went on to possibly create other casualties through their mistaken beliefs. True faith brings forth good and even powerful works that attract people to Christ. Presumption and fanaticism bring Christ and His followers into ridicule and disrepute, driving people away from faith and into cynicism about Christianity. Just think of the stigma brought upon all Bible-believing Christians by those who refuse to allow their children to receive lifesaving medical treatment because of their extreme beliefs regarding divine healing. It is important that we have a right and balanced understanding of our authority.

As we have seen, it is a mistake to treat healing in the same way as forgiveness or deliverance from demonic bondage, because the fallen, natural order is still with us. So how should we view healing? We should view both healing and miracles as signs pointing to Christ's total and coming victory. They are signs that the future kingdom of God is near at hand and can break into our present time. They tell us that the corruption of this world is not the final reality, that a day is coming when all evil and corruption will be destroyed. As signs, they point beyond themselves to a destination that we have not yet reached, but we are on the way. They point us to God's love and compassion.

All of us should rejoice when someone is healed and receive it as a gift and sign that God is among us. And when we aren't healed, we should lean into God's grace and encourage ourselves in the knowledge that God has a plan to bring good out of every situation for those who love Him.[135]

Signs, wonders, and healings have another important role. They catch the unbeliever's attention to listen to the wonderful gospel message. The New Testament emphasizes the importance of healings and miracles as signs that lead people to belief.[136] In God's plan, they serve as signs to draw people's attention and help authenticate God's gospel message. Let us always be faithful in this wonderful ministry of praying for the healing of the sick. Let us also remember that while we have **already** been given the kingdom, we have **not yet** received it in its fullness.

---

[135] Romans 8:28
[136] John 3:2; John 10:25, 37-38; Acts 4:29-30

Chapter 9

God's Extraordinary Times

I shall remember the deeds of the Lord; surely I will remember Your wonders of Old.   *- Psalm 77:11*

One feature of God's mighty works is that they are not spread throughout history equally. A study of the Bible reveals that there are seasons when God's mighty works are very numerous and apparent. We might think of these as extraordinary times as compared to more ordinary times. The most unique of these eras is when God is establishing something new. **God's most powerful works are concentrated around three main events:**

- **The Creation of the Universe** out of nothing by God's Word.
- **The Creation of Israel** by means of the Exodus, the giving of the Law, and the conquest of Canaan
- **The Creation of the Church** through the coming of Jesus, the inauguration of the gospel, and the coming of the Holy Spirit at Pentecost.

Anyone reading the Bible can't help but notice that at these three times, God stepped out from behind the curtain and took things very powerfully into His own hands. Miraculous events took place that are not seen in more normal times.

In the Creation account, God speaks, and stars and planets appear out of nothing, dry land appears on earth, animals and humans are created, and God visits with Adam daily in the Garden and speaks to him directly.

During the Exodus period, great, miraculous plagues mysteriously appear to force the Egyptians to release the Israelites, God leads them in a fiery pillar, the Red Sea splits into two, manna appears every morning, the walls of Jericho collapse, and many other miracles happen.

In the Gospels and Acts we read of Jesus healing every person who comes to Him for healing, 5,000 people are fed with five loaves and two fishes, Jesus walks on water, the Holy Spirit is poured out as flames of fire, the dead are raised, and people are healed by Peter's shadow.

In all these instances, God powerfully broke through in extraordinary ways. These were not normal times but were unique in God's dealings in human history. We must keep this fact in mind as we read our Bibles. It will help temper us from being dogmatic.

Living in Ordinary Times

Some point out that Jesus is our example and we never see an instance of Jesus praying for a physical healing that did not occur. They also point to people being raised from the dead in New Testament times by Jesus and the apostles. They say that if only we had more faith or had more boldness we would see the same results. I heard a speaker say once that we needed to apologize to all the sick around us since the only reason they are sick or crippled is because we lack the faith to heal them. But is this true? Are they right?

Well, for one thing they are overlooking a key fact: Jesus was and is the King. Wherever He went, the kingdom of God was fully present, and therefore everyone who came to Him was healed. Sickness could not stand against the full presence of the kingdom of God. Only Jesus could do this because only Jesus brought heaven to earth completely. We are to imitate Him, but He carried more authority than you or I ever could.

The apostles were also one of a kind. Tremendous signs, wonders, and healings surrounded their ministries. They were uniquely selected as the 12 men that Jesus trained personally for their assignment. These were chosen men who lived in an extraordinary time and were given a unique role. Like Jesus, they performed astonishing signs and wonders to authenticate their message and bring forth and establish something brand new: The Church.

How will we escape if we neglect so great a salvation? After it was at the first spoken through the Lord, it was confirmed to us by those who heard [the apostles], God also testifying with them, both by signs and wonders and by various miracles and by gifts of the Holy Spirit, according to His own will.
- Hebrews 2:3-4

We can deny the erroneous teaching that the gifts of the Spirit and the age of miracles passed away with the death of the last apostle and at the same time recognize that they were absolutely unique men who carried an authority beyond what any of us have. Revelation 21:14 tells us that the twelve apostles are the foundation stones of the city of God which comes down out of heaven. It was these same apostles (and their personal associates) that gave us the books of the New Testament. After they were gone, no more writings were included.

It is right that we should take Jesus and the apostles as our examples and strive to be like them, but it is unrealistic that we should expect that our ministry and experience will match theirs. They were unique men who lived at a unique time. We have never again seen an explosion of miracles like we see in the Gospels and the Book of Acts. Failure to understand this can lead us into great disappointment and discouragement or, worse yet, ungrounded fanaticism. It is proper humility to recognize that God sets the times and seasons and determines the characteristics of each season. There are other times when the kingdom of God draws especially near, however, and God's activity increases. We call these times "revival."

What Is a Revival?

Will You not Yourself revive us again, that Your people may rejoice in You? Show us Your lovingkindness, O Lord, and grant us Your salvation   - Psalm 85:6-7

During a time of spiritual and social decline in Israel, the psalmist prays for God to bring a revival, or spiritual quickening, to His people. A careful reading of the Bible shows the history of God's people as a series of long, slow, spiritual declines followed by brief periods of powerful revivals sent from God.

A revival is a divine interruption in the normal course of spiritual matters. It is the Lord stepping forward and revealing Himself through extraordinary conviction and acts of power. In times of true revival, human personalities withdraw to the background as God takes center stage and propels His kingdom forward.

In Israel's history, there were powerful revivals under Moses[137] and Joshua.[138] Then there were eight cycles of decline and revival during the 400 years recorded in the Book of Judges, each led by a judge/deliverer that God raised up, such as Gideon. There were also powerful revivals under Samuel,[139] Solomon,[140] Elijah,[141] Jehoiada,[142] Hezekiah,[143] and Ezra.[144] There were other revivals in the Old Testament and some, no doubt, that were not recorded.

The greatest revival was in the New Testament, first under John the Baptist and Jesus[145] and then on the Day of Pentecost under the apostles.[146]

We can say that all progress in true religion comes as a result of revival. It seems that human nature, being what it is, always leads to eventual decline apart from God's intervention. Human societies, as well as individuals, have an inherent gravity due to human pride that saps the spiritual vitality and brings decline. You can see this same pattern throughout Church history. God's kingdom does

---

[137] Exodus 4:27-31
[138] Joshua 24:14-18
[139] 1 Samuel 7:3-10
[140] 1 Kings 8:10-11, 55-56, 65
[141] 1 Kings 18:36-39
[142] 2 Kings 11:17-21
[143] 2 Kings 18:1-8
[144] Ezra 8-10
[145] Matthew 3:4-6; John 3:24-26
[146] Acts 2. There were other revivals in other cities mentioned in the Book of Acts as well.

not just simply advance through slow, steady progress. Rather, history shows periods of stagnation, then decline followed by sudden, great advances due to revivals, which carry everything forward for some years until stagnation again sets in.

It's true that an individual can have a personal revival, as can a family or a church. The most powerful revivals, however, affect whole cities and even nations.

The prophet Isaiah prayed during a difficult time in Israel's history when the nation was in a spiritually backslidden state and surrounded by threatening foreign powers. Isaiah prayed that God would come down with revival power.

> *Oh, that You would rend the heavens and come down, that the mountains might quake at Your presence—as fire kindles the brushwood, as fire causes water to boil—to make Your name known to Your adversaries, that the nations may tremble at Your presence! - Isaiah 64:1-2*

A revival means that God *"comes down"* and acts decisively. Isaiah's prayer was answered some years later with the great revival under Hezekiah that we referred to above.

The revival that began in Jerusalem on the day of Pentecost—recorded in the second chapter of Acts—was the greatest revival of all time. On that day, Jesus sent the Holy Spirit from heaven and there were great manifestations. There was the sound of a mighty, rushing wind. Tongues that looked like fire appeared over the disciples. They spoke in languages they did not know and were therefore able to preach the gospel to all the foreign speakers who had gathered in Jerusalem to celebrate this great festival. On that day, 3,000 men were converted to Christ. In the days, weeks, and months that followed, there were mighty miracles, healings, and signs as tens of thousands came to Christ. God had come down with power. The Holy Spirit brought a powerful awareness of the reality of God and a profound sense of the people's sinfulness and need. In the years and decades that followed, the Church of Jesus Christ was powerfully established across the Roman Empire as the revival spread.

Revivals in America

America has been blessed with many revivals. Some have been so powerful, have affected so many people, and have brought about such profound societal change that they are known as Great Awakenings.

The First Great Awakening took place between the years 1734 and 1742, prior to which the Church was in a weakened state. Although many of the earliest arrivals came to America with a fervent vision for establishing a godly nation, such as the pilgrims and puritans, within less than a century the spiritual ardor of the Americans had cooled. The focus had instead shifted to increasing wealth. The Enlightenment with its anti-religious bias had made great inroads into the colleges and among the educated classes. New waves of immigrants came who did not hold to the evangelical, Protestant faith. Churches were largely empty, and ministers were greatly concerned and began to pray intensely. God answered with a great revival.

Although there were earlier stirrings, the First Great Awakening is generally dated as beginning in 1734 in New England, under the preaching of Jonathan Edwards in

Massachusetts. The Awakening gradually spread around the colonies and peaked around 1740, under the preaching of George Whitefield and John and Charles Wesley. The whole countryside seemed to be aflame, and huge outdoor crowds gathered together to hear the preaching of George Whitefield and the Wesleys. Huge numbers were saved amidst great demonstrations of the Holy Spirit's conviction. Denominational walls were overcome, and there was a great harvest of evangelism. In New England alone, church membership increased from 25,000 to 50,000 from 1740-1742.[147] Hundreds of churches were formed to make room for all the converts. There was an extended "afterglow" that lasted another decade, in which the churches continued to grow. As a result, positive moral and social changes took place and the colonies were united together.

Following the War for Independence, the churches had again fallen into a low state, partially as a result of the ravages of the war and the re-emergence of Enlightenment thinking from England and France. Once again, the pastors and church leaders were alarmed, and the churches began to pray for a new visitation from God. The Second Great Awakening began to stir in the 1790s, spreading far wider than the first, reaching even to the western frontier. It "transformed Kentucky and Tennessee from an utterly lawless community into a God-fearing one."[148] The Second Great Awakening was actually a series of hundreds of revivals that gradually spread to every corner of our country over a period of 35 years, touching every class. Church

---

[147] "What was the Great Awakening?"
https://www.christianity.com/church/church-history/timeline/1701-1800/the-great-awakening-11630212.html
[148] The Fervent Prayer, J Edwin Orr, Moody Press, 1974 pg xiv

membership exploded. For instance, the fledging Baptist Church grew from 95,000 members in 1800 to 160,000 in 1810, and the Methodist Church grew by 167.8% in the same ten year period.[149] Over a million people are believed to have been converted during this time, and the changes in society were profound. Movements for the abolition of slavery, women's rights, prison reform, education, and other social reforms were created and grew rapidly. The atmosphere on our nation's colleges was transformed.

Another most remarkable nationwide revival took place in 1858-59. A layman named Jeremy Lanphier advertised a daily lunchtime prayer meeting in downtown New York for September 23, 1857, and on the first day only six people showed up. In the second week there was a great financial panic among the businessmen of New York, and the prayer meeting's attendance skyrocketed.

And then something remarkable happened. The prayer meeting continued to grow and multiply across the business district. Within six months, 10,000 businessmen were gathering across New York every day to pray for America.[150] Soon, evening meetings were held in all of the churches, with scores coming to Christ. By June of 1858 (just nine months after the first prayer meeting), the publication *Presbyterian Magazine* reported there had been 50,000 converts in New York out of a total population of 800,000 (If you remove from the total population those who were already saved, you see how large a percentage of the unsaved population this was).[151] News of this great

---

[149] Revival and Revivalism, Iain H. Murray, Banner of Truth Publishing, 2002 pgs 116-117
[150] Orr pgs 4-5
[151] Orr p9

revival spread like wildfire across the country, and prayer meetings sprang up all across America. It is widely estimated that one million people came to Christ in just one year.

The great Pentecostal Revival is generally marked as beginning in 1906 in a small building on Azusa Street in Los Angeles, California. For the next three and a half years they had meetings three times a day with tens of thousands of visitors from all over the globe coming to experience Pentecostal power.[152] These visitors spread the revival across the whole world. By the year 2000, there were 582 million Christians who are descendants of that revival.[153]

Beginning in the late 1960s and lasting throughout most of the 1970s was a revival known as the Jesus Movement, or the Charismatic Renewal. During a very turbulent time in our nation's history, when our society was being rent apart by the sexual revolution, the anti-war movement, the emergence of drugs, and several assassinations of national leaders,[154] God broke in. The revival began quietly in a grassroots movement until it gripped our nation. This revival had three main expressions: First, the conversion of hippies, street people, and other disaffected youth. Second, a revival among students in our nation's colleges. And third, the charismatic renewal among churches. Many of the great churches, denominations, parachurch organizations, and mission groups in America today were formed or multiplied during this revival. Both my brother and I were saved

---

[152] As in all revivals, there was great repentance among those who attended.

[153] Jenkins, Philip. "The Next Christendom" Oxford Press, 3rd Edition, 2011. Pg. 80

[154] Between 1963 and 1968 President John Kennedy, his brother Robert Kennedy (who was running for the Democratic nomination to be president), and civil rights leader Martin Luther King Jr. were all assassinated.

through it, as were many leaders in churches all over America. Millions were saved across America.

Our nation has had a number of other notable religious movements and city-wide revivals under such people as Charles Finney, D.L Moody, Billy Sunday, Billy Graham, and others. Also there have been powerful revivals that have swept through individual churches.

Our church has had several seasons of revival that have transformed the atmosphere and culture of our community and transformed many lives. The most powerful one took place 25 years ago. We caught a powerful revival flame from visiting a church in Canada, and it spread quickly throughout our church. Our first night home we held a church-wide meeting, and the power of God fell dramatically. My brother Dave had a word of knowledge to call all the kids forward. When we prayed for them, every single one was filled with the Holy Spirit and they wept under the love of God. After the weeping, they were filled with the joy of the Lord and remained transfixed in the Lord's presence for over an hour. It was the greatest demonstration of God's power I have ever witnessed.

For the next five months we met five nights a week as thousands of people came to experience the revival. Many were saved and many lives and marriages were transformed. A number who were touched by that revival went into full and part-time ministry. Perhaps most notably, an anointing for working with children and youth was released in our church. In the years since then we have worked with tens of thousands of young people locally and around the world, most notably in Kenya and Uganda.[155]

When Revival Ebbs

One thing is for sure; a revival never lasts forever. Few visitations and revivals last more than a few years. After the revival follows an "afterglow" period in which very significant evangelism and positive social changes continue to take place. These periods can last for several decades as the recently saved and revived Christians continue to advance the cause of Christ and righteousness before stagnation sets in. Each of these cycles advances Christ's Church farther than it had ever been before.

When the initial revival begins to lift, the extreme manifestations of God and the number of healings and miracles begin to lessen as well. We begin to enter more normal times. This is simply a law or reality of revivals. When people do not recognize this, or refuse to accept it, they fall into the trap of trying to hype back the revival manifestations with carnal excesses, manipulation, and fleshly, psychic works. They may even begin to accept demonic manifestations. To my knowledge, there never was a revival that was not followed by a period where some of the people went off into unbiblical extremes. Some movements in the Church today are destructive wildfires begun from the waning embers of the Charismatic Renewal.

---

[155] Currently we operate 5 area community teen centers, 4 Christian schools, Christian clubs in 35 area public elementary, middle and high schools, a Sunday morning bus ministry, a large annual youth conference and huge ministries to youth in Africa with 70,000 involved.

False Revival Fire

I remember reading where one of the old time revival leaders said, "When a revival is beginning Satan stands in its way and does everything he can to stop it through persecution, but if that fails, then he runs around to the back of the wagon and tries to push it as fast as he can into error and excess."

Gardiner Spring, a leading revivalist of the Second Great Awakening, put it this way:

> *There is nothing [the devil] is so much afraid of as the power of the Holy Ghost. Where he cannot arrest the showers of blessing, it has ever been one of his devices to dilute or poison the streams...This he does, not so much by opposing them, but by counterfeiting the genuine coin, by getting up revivals that are spurious and to his liking.[156]*

These excesses only multiply as the authentic revival begins to wane.

Jonathan Edwards states that one of the things that ended the First Great Awakening was the rise of people with what he called "enthusiastic delusions."[157] These were leaders who claimed great supernatural powers and whipped people up into frenzied, emotional states. Two such men were James Davenport, a minister in Southold, New York, and Benjamin Pomeroy of New York. Their extreme antics and meetings introduced great confusion

---

[156] Gardiner Spring, Personal Reminiscences of the Life and Times of Gardener Spring (New York, 1866), vol. 1, pp. 217-18
[157] "A Faithful Narrative of the Surprising Work of God"- Baker Book House, 1979. pg 96.

and division and brought the revival into disrepute.[158]

Near the end of the Second Great Awakening, extremist "revivalists" held wild "revival meetings" in western and central New York. These revivals were so extreme and brought religion into such disrepute as to create a district that the great evangelist Charles Finney would later coin as "The Burned Over District," a name that has stuck. The term referred to ground that had been burned over so thoroughly that it became difficult for later, true revivals to take root.

> *There had been a few years previously, a wild excitement passing through that region, which they called a revival of religion, but which turned out to be spurious...It was reported as having been a very extravagant excitement; and resulted in a (public) reaction so extensive and profound, as to leave the impression on many minds that religion was a mere delusion.*[159]

Frank Bartleman, one of the leaders of the great Pentecostal Revival at Azusa Street, noted that although they received great persecution and also scandalous reports from the press, they had a far greater hindrance. It was false ministers with false manifestations who tried to join the movement:

> *Outside persecution never hurt the work. We had the most to fear from the workings of evil spirits within. Even spiritualists*

---

[158] In July of 1744, Davenport published a retraction of his views and actions claiming that he had been possessed by "demonic spirits."
[159] Finney, Charles. The Memoirs of Charles G. Finney. Zondervan 2002. Chapter 6, Page 61

and hypnotists came to investigate, and to try their influence.
Then all the religious soreheads, crooks, and cranks came,
seeking a place in the work.[160]

Unfortunately, these false revivals often spawn cults and false movements that remain with us today.

Revival is a time of widespread spiritual awakening, of conviction of sins, of repentance, and a new and better direction being set for the Church, city, or country. It is a time of men and women becoming ignited for Christ. Whenever God's people are in a weakened state and are being oppressed, the hunger for revival increases. In such times people look eagerly for any sign of revival to give them hope.

One danger of this is that people can be so desirous of revival that they can naively accept spurious claims of revival conditions. Sometimes unscrupulous individuals even manipulate others with trickery, psychological manipulation, and exaggerated or false stories to build their name and reputation as powerful revivalists. This has been a recurring problem for the Church since the very beginning. Jesus warned of those who, though seeming to have powerful ministries, would seek to mislead us.

For false messiahs and false prophets will appear and
perform great signs and wonders to deceive, if possible, even
the elect.   - Matthew 24:24, NIV

The New Testament talks about such men as Simon of Samaria, who performed great acts of magic that astonished

---

160 Bartleman, Frank. Compiled by Liardon, Roberts. Frank Bartleman's Azusa Street. Destiny Image Publishers, Apr. 1, 2006. Chapter Two.

the people, who was baptized and joined the Church, but was later rebuked by Peter for his perverse motivation.[161] Paul, while traveling through Cyprus, encountered a false Jewish prophet named Bar-Jesus who practiced magic and sorcery and attempted to deceive those Paul was trying to reach, until Paul publicly rebuked him.[162]

The Core Problem of Lawlessness

At the heart of false revival and false manifestations is lawlessness. This is the attitude that will not submit your will, understanding, and agenda to God's will, understanding, and agenda. A lawless spirit won't trust what God in His wisdom has for us. It won't wait on His timing but demands everything now, often before we are ready. It does not defer to and follow those that Jesus has appointed but rather seeks attention and grasps for position.

Many people proclaim themselves as Christians but are actually lawless individuals. Unfortunately, this can be true for some ministers–even those who claim a signs-and-wonders ministry. Jesus warned us of such lawless individuals.

Not everyone who says to Me, "Lord, Lord," will enter the kingdom of heaven, but He who does the will of My Father who is in heaven will enter. Many will say to Me on that day, "Lord, Lord, did we not prophesy in Your name, and in Your name cast out demons, and in Your name perform

---

161 Acts 8:9-11, 13, 18-21. Early Church leaders such as Justin Martyr and Irenaeus write that Simon later went on to form a false cult called the Simonists
162 Acts 12:5-12 See also Acts 16:16-18 regarding false spirits trying to identify with Christ's followers

many miracles?" And then I will declare to them, "I never knew you; depart from Me, you who practice lawlessness."
- Matthew 7:21-23

Now, the source of these prophecies, deliverances, and miracles is not defined. Were they just illusions done by unscrupulous people manipulating their audiences? Were they demonic works done with Satan's power? Or were they actual works of the Holy Spirit done in response to the faith and need of people who came for healing and deliverance—despite the unworthiness of the ministers? Jesus doesn't tell us. What we do know is that these people were false ministers because they were lawless. In other words, they did not do *"the will of My Father who is in heaven."*

My friend Charles Simpson likes to say that a false prophet is not merely one whose prophecies fail to come to pass but also one that the Lord has not sent or appointed.[163] Because they are not sent, they will bring forth wildfire. They will not bring the fruit of the Lord.

In fact, the actions and ministries of lawless individuals actually cause people's love to grow cold as those being influenced become more lawless themselves.

Many false prophets will arise and will mislead many. Because lawlessness is increased, most people's love will grow cold. - Matthew 24:11-12

The word translated "love" is the Greek word "agape," which is a word the Bible only applies to the followers of Christ. Lawless ministry causes Christians' love to grow colder rather than causing them to love Jesus, His

---

[163] Jeremiah 14:14, 23:21 (NIV), 32

followers, and the lost more. Following the lead of the lawless minister, their focus drifts away from Jesus and focuses on themselves more and more.

A lawless spirit is inward focused and has great ambitions for itself. It is the drive to be admired, to be the center of attention. It's why when we are young we dream of being rock stars, movie stars, and sports celebrities. Coming to Christ does not by itself deal with this drive for attention and approval. It can express itself even through our ministry. It can lead people, even ministers, to boast, exaggerate, and mislead people in order to build up their reputations and esteem.[164] The desire to be a movie or sports celebrity can easily mutate into striving to be a spiritual celebrity.

You see, at its core, lawlessness can lead people to take glory due to God and redirect it to themselves. Of course, this is a dangerous path to go down and leads to self-delusion. This is certainly one of the main reasons why so many "spiritual celebrities" in the charismatic world have fallen into sin and dishonor. Jesus taught us that humbling ourselves is the path to God exalting us but that self-promotion and efforts to exalt ourselves lead to dishonor and humiliation.[165] We live in a lawless age under the influence of humanistic, self-focused psychology and New Age spirituality. For this reason we must be alert to false leaders and movements.

So what are the marks of a true revival? With so many claiming to be revivalists, it is important to know the signs. Let's take Acts 2 as the model.

---

[164] The more insecure a person is, the more likely they are to stretch the truth in their stories and testimonies to win approval and acclaim.
[165] Luke 14:11

The Marks of True Revival

First, it began with a sovereign move of God pouring out the Holy Spirit with great power and remarkable works. The revival on Pentecost began with signs and wonders: tongues as of fire and the sound of a mighty, rushing wind. These would soon be joined by tremendous healings.

So the **first mark** of a true revival is that God sovereignly draws near and does extraordinary things. A revival is not something we can work up with emotion and zeal. It is God "coming down."

Next, after a crowd gathered, Peter stood up to preach.[166] His message centered on the gospel message of what Jesus had done and the salvation being offered. In 11 of the 23 verses of his sermon, Peter quotes from the Old Testament. In the last two verses of his sermon, He calls the people to repentance and salvation.

So the **second mark** of true revivals is that they feature biblical preaching that is focused on Jesus and the gospel, and includes a call to repentance and salvation.

Therefore, any so-called revival or move of God that doesn't center on Jesus above all, and which downplays the role of biblical preaching of the gospel and a call to repentance, is suspect, to say the least.

The **third mark** that follows from this is that all true revivals are marked by deep conviction and powerful repentance. Note the effect of Peter's preaching on the unbelieving Jews:

---

[166] Acts 2:14

Now when they heard this, they were pierced to the heart, and said to Peter and the rest of the apostles, "Brethren, what shall we do?" Peter said to them, "Repent, and each of you be baptized in the name of Jesus Christ for the forgiveness of your sins; and you will receive the gift of the Holy Spirit"
- Acts 2:37-38

Revivals are intended to win the lost and reform believers to be more like the God Who is visiting them in holiness. This means that there must be deep repentance displayed.

The fourth mark is that many people are won to Christ. On that day, as we noted earlier, 3,000 were saved.[167] Many so-called revival meetings today are not winning great numbers to the Lord, nor are they making Christians more holy. When we study true revivals, we find that the most of the converts go on to become very strong Christians and that holiness is greatly elevated in the Church. Sexual immorality, greed, and other sins are largely washed from the Church.

A fifth mark of revivals is that they increase love and unity among believers. The Jerusalem church grew in love and sharing what they had with each other and devoted themselves to the apostles' teaching.[168] So every revival should make the Church healthier, with respect for spiritual authority and a renewed focus of apostolic doctrine, which is contained in the New Testament. It should leave behind an atmosphere where God is free to work.

Every true revival or move of God should produce these same things. We can test a claim that a revival is

---

[167] Acts 2:41
[168] Acts 2:41-43

happening by whether these five marks are present.

In looking around at our troubled culture today, every one of us should be stirred to pray for revival and for another awakening. We can all encourage ourselves with the knowledge that America, despite all her faults, is only one heaven-sent awakening away from once more truly being "One Nation under God." God has done it in our past, and He certainly wants to do it in our future. One of the great promises Jesus gave us was: *"I will build My church; and the Gates of Hades [Hell] will not overpower it."*[169] What a great comfort to know that Jesus has taken the initiative to build the Church and guarantees that it will succeed and triumph over all other powers. He has given us the power of the Holy Spirit, along with His gifts, and even sends us special seasons of unusual power to accomplish it. We should always yield to His Spirit, actively use His gifts, and pray for the special seasons of revival He sends. America desperately needs another great revival.

God certainly has wonderful things ahead for His Church. In the next chapter, we will look at the incredible truth of how Jesus will use you to build His glorious Church and how you can become His instrument for revival.

---

[169] Matthew 16:18

Chapter 10
Looking Ahead

That the God of our Lord Jesus Christ, the Father of glory, may give to you a spirit of wisdom and of revelation in the knowledge of Him. I pray that the eyes of your heart may be enlightened, so that you will know what is the hope of His calling, what are the riches of the glory of His inheritance in the saints, and what is the surpassing greatness of His power toward us who believe. - Ephesians 1:17-19

Paul prays that we would receive a revelation that will make us the kind of Christians the world needs today. People are looking for spiritual reality and supernatural help. They find it in churches that believe the Bible and rely on the power of the Holy Spirit and His gifts to bring healing and deliverance. These churches are changing lives and changing the world!

The Pentecostal/Charismatic form of Christianity is the fastest-growing movement in the world. Beginning in Los Angeles in a small chapel on Azusa Street in 1906, it has spread internationally 582 adherents by 2000 and is expected to reach 800 million by 2025.[170] Even in America, Pentecostal/Charismatic Christianity continues to thrive. While liberal mainline churches have declined precipitously

---

[170] "The Next Christendom," Philip Jenkins, Oxford Press, 3rd ed, 2011, Page 80

over the past 60 years, those who claim to be Pentecostal or charismatic had grown to 36% of the population by 2008.[171]

Churches where people encounter the power of God will continue to grow. If we want to see our friends and neighbors come to Christ and we want to see America turned and transformed, we can only do it by the power of the Holy Spirit. This means every one of us must learn how to live in the Holy Spirit's power.

In this final chapter, we will look expectantly towards the future God invites us to live in. We will study how to discover and exercise our spiritual gifts, and how to live by the Holy Spirit's power each day. We will discover the secret of a fruitful and adventurous life that comes from following the Holy Spirit's leading. Finally, we will learn how to recognize and prepare for those seasons, or extraordinary times, of revival and renewal that God sends us to accomplish His purpose. I hope you are as excited as I am about what God has planned!

Putting the Gifts to Work

As more Christians learn to walk in the Spirit's power, we will see greater victories. I like to say that **the Church's problem is not a supply problem but an unemployment problem.** The apostle Peter tells us:

As each one has received a special gift, employ it in serving one another as good stewards of the manifold grace of God.
- 1 Peter 4:10

---

[171] Study by the Barna Research Group cited in The Christian Post, Church and Ministries, "Myths Exposed on Charismatic Christianity" in America, January 7, 2008. This number includes those Charismatic Christians who remain in Catholic, mainline, and Evangelical denominations.

As we saw in chapters 5 and 6, every Christian has received a spiritual gift, something of great value to build up the Church and reach the lost. Here Peter tells us that we must put that gift to work. Unfortunately, not every Christian is employed in using their gift. The truth is, if we solved our unemployment problem in the Church, and every Christian was operating in the power and gifting of the Holy Spirit, then nothing could stop the Church.

Sadly, many churches have become places where a just a few people actually do the ministry and most others just watch them. My friend Charles Simpson has said, "Many churches have become a theater instead of a family with a mission." In other words, many Christians flock to church on Sunday to watch a theatrical presentation with skilled musicians, entertaining and humorous speakers, high-quality light and sound systems, and engaging video presentations. But when they leave the church and go home, they do not live Spirit-empowered, overcoming lives. Now, there is nothing wrong with having excellence in our weekend services, but it is essential that we are being trained and sent out to live fruitful and effective lives.

Because of wrong priorities, unbelief, and fear, many believers do not live such Spirit-empowered lives. They are not advancing Christ's kingdom much. So here are two questions we all must ask ourselves:

- Do I believe the Bible when it says that I have been given a divinely empowered gift?
- Am I willing to employ it?

You may ask, "But how do I know what my spiritual gift is?" Remember, in chapter 6, we talked about the **function gifts, listed in Romans 12,** which establish our role or function in the Body of Christ. We said that these are like our job descriptions. They are prophecy, service, teaching, exhortation, giving, leadership, and showing mercy.

We also studied **the manifestation gifts of 1 Corinthians 12.** We saw that these are manifestations of God's power and knowledge given to us as needed, as we operate in our function gifts. Therefore, we are to *discover* what our functional gift is and *pray for* the manifestation gifts as the Holy Spirit sees we need them.[172]

To find your function gift, look for opportunities to serve. As you minister and serve in a variety of ways and settings, you will find that certain areas of ministry appeal to you more and give you more joy. You will also notice that God seems to use you more effectively in that ministry. You may also feel a special measure of the compassion and power of God flowing through you to others. People will recognize God's blessing on your efforts in that area and will comment on it. You may receive prophecies from others that confirm it as your area of gifting.

When I was a young Christian I volunteered in many different areas, wanting to help out in the church. Over time, my area of gifting became evident. We should be willing to help in any area that is needed but at the same time recognize that God has made each of us a specialist in some area of His grace and concentrate in that area.

Be sure to talk to your pastor or some mature Christian who knows you well. They have probably already noticed your area of gifting. It is important that

---

[172] You may want to go back and reread chapters 5 and 6 if you are not yet clear about spiritual gifts or have questions.

your notion of your function gift is also recognized and ordained by church leaders. This is more important than any notion you have or any prophecy someone gives you. Recognizing and ordaining people's gifts and readiness for ministry is one of the most important roles for pastors and elders. When people ignore this step, confusion, disappointment, and vexation can result.

Rediscovering our Great Helper

If you are to be truly effective and fruitful, you must learn to draw from the Holy Spirit who empowers you. The Christian life is lived in, by, and through the Holy Spirit. He motivates, encourages, and empowers us. He is our constant Helper. The Holy Spirit is not just a force or power, He is the third Person in the Trinity. Let me ask you this: What is your relationship with the Holy Spirit like?

When Jesus, after spending three years with His disciples, was about to leave them and ascend to heaven, He said something crucially important.

> *I will ask the Father, and He will give you another Helper, that He may be with you forever; that is the Spirit of truth, whom the world cannot receive, because it does not see Him or know Him, but you know Him because He abides with you and will be in you. I will not leave you as orphans; I will come to you. - John 14:16, 18*

The Holy Spirit had abided among them in the person of Jesus, but soon He would be sent to live in them (and us). Notice that Jesus referred to Him as a Helper. He has been given to us to help us. The Greek word translated as Helper here is *"Paraclete."* It comes from two Greek words "*kaleo*" which means "to call" and "*para*" which translates as "beside" or "alongside of." So the Holy Spirit has been called to walk with or alongside us. He is our Helper who is always present with us. So let me ask you again: What is your relationship with the Holy Spirit like?"

Every day you see people checking their smartphones. You can consult it for information as well as directions. You can use it to reach out to someone for encouragement and advice, and if you get in trouble, you can call for help. I have found it to be a great help, and I use it many times each day. You are never really alone if you have your phone with you.

Many Christians who use their smartphone every day forget that Jesus has given them a far greater Helper who is with them. **Do you truly know the Holy Spirit as your Helper? What part does He play in your life? How often during the day do you turn to Him and rely on Him?** Remember He is called to walk alongside you and give you help. All day long, through every challenge and opportunity, He is with you to help, strengthen, and comfort you.

Harald Bredesen was a man with an amazing life story. Noted author and *New York Times* editor Bob Slosser called him "the minister to world leaders."[173] Many others called him "heaven's ambassador," and he was certainly that. Friend and spiritual advisor to three U.S. presidents, as well as foreign presidents, kings, and royalty, God used him in the most unlikely and incredible ways. He was credited with coining the term "Charismatic Renewal" and mentored many of the movement's leaders. He led Pat Robertson into the baptism of the Holy Spirit and mentored him. Pat

---

[173] Bob Slosser Reagan Inside/Out.

even served for a time as assistant pastor at the church Harald was pastoring before he went out and founded the Christian Broadcasting Network. Harald literally impacted the world, yet he never built a large ministry or organization. His secret was simply in following the leading of the Holy Spirit every day into the most amazing divine appointments.

Towards the end of his life, Harald befriended me and we spent many days together. I learned his secret the first day that I met him. Harald talked with God throughout the day. In whatever we did, he was communicating with his heavenly Father, Jesus, and the Holy Spirit. He would thank God for every blessing (no matter how small), rejoice with Him in every victory, ask for His help in every challenge, and intercede for the people we came in contact with. It was clear he enjoyed having the Holy Spirit as his Helper and was always ready for the next adventure. Harald's example should inspire all of us to be more aware of the Holy Spirit's presence in our lives.

Leaning into the Holy Spirit

Years ago when we were starting our church, a friend named Lonnie Frisbee shared with us the concept of "leaning into the Holy Spirit."[174] **Since the Holy Spirit is always with us to help and strengthen us, we can simply lean into or lean upon Him for help.**

When you are a young pastor, you are constantly having to do things for the first time, things you feel completely inexperienced and unprepared for. You must preach to

---

[174] Lonnie Frisbee was one of the leading figures of the Jesus Movement and was known as the "hippie preacher." He moved powerfully in the Holy Spirit and influenced tens of thousands of people, including many leaders.

crowds, comfort those who have lost loved ones, conduct funerals, counsel people, cast out demons, and much more. As a young pastor you are vitally aware that you lack the experience and wisdom necessary, and yet God has called you to do it. Therefore, we had to learn to lean confidently upon the One who could help us.

You see, your confidence is not in yourself but in the One who will supply whatever is needed through you. You say to the Holy Spirit, **"I feel totally inadequate and don't know what I am doing, but You have called me to do this, and I will now lean into Your promised help and enablement."** Rather than being timid and afraid, you step out and discover the wisdom, love, and power of the Holy Spirit flowing through you.

If Jesus has called you to be a parent, spouse, or ministry leader, then you can count on the Holy Spirit to back, equip, and empower you to be fruitful and effective. Likewise, He has called you to be the salt and light in your workplace, neighborhood, school, and in numerous other settings. He will give you His powerful help in all these roles. He wants you to succeed and be effective. You do not have to be afraid, and that ought to boost your confidence tremendously!

The Bible tells us to develop the skill of looking to the Lord in every circumstance.

Trust in the Lord with all your heart, and lean not on your own understanding; in all your ways acknowledge Him, and He shall direct your paths. - *Proverbs 3:5-6, NKJV*

We are promised that if we will acknowledge the Lord's priority in all the events of life, and trust Him enough to truly follow Him, then we can be assured that He will lead us and direct our paths. Sometimes this may mean we have a dream or vision that tells us what to do, but more often we will have to trust in His invisible guidance and His inner strengthening and wisdom.[175]

This hour-by-hour leaning into the Lord's promised supply is also known as "walking by the Spirit." [176] As you know, walking involves many small steps. In the same way, walking by the Spirit involves making small adjustments throughout the day to continue to lean into the Holy Spirit as we encounter the challenges of each day.

This requires staying in touch with the Holy Spirit throughout the day. As we encounter each challenge or opportunity, we can send up a silent prayer of "I yield to You. Help me to have Jesus' attitude here," "Let me have Your eyes to see the opportunities to glorify Christ in this situation," or "Give me Your wisdom and strength for this challenge," etc. When it's over, simply acknowledge your gratitude for His help.

Renewing Your Mind

In order to "walk by the Spirit," we must first adjust our mindset.

> *So that the requirement of the Law might be fulfilled in us, who do not walk according to the flesh but according to the Spirit. For those who are according to the flesh set their*

---

[175] The Bible promises us that if we need wisdom and ask God in faith we can be assured the wisdom will be supplied. See James 1:5.

[176] Galatians 5:25

minds on the things of the flesh, but those who are according to the Spirit, the things of the Spirit.   - Romans 8:4-5

If we set our mind on the things of the Spirit, we will tend to walk by the Spirit. **Thinking precedes acting. What you think and meditate on is what you will draw from.** Our thoughts should be focused on the mission and glory of Jesus and also on the Word of God. These are certainly the "things of the Spirit."[177]

Sometimes people claim that we should not be so focused on the Bible when we have the author of the Bible present with us. They say, "We may miss what the Spirit is saying today if we make an idol out of what He said 2,000 years ago." They even have a word for it–"Bibliolatry"–that is, to make an idol of the Bible. However, this is a false dichotomy. The tension is not between the Bible and the Spirit, the tension is between the Bible and subjectivism.[178] Having a high view of the Bible and deferring to it never hinders the working of the Holy Spirit, but it sure puts a check on a wild imagination, unbridled emotions, and faulty teaching.

God wants us to be confident and joyously expectant as we seek the gifts and empowerment of the Holy Spirit. We have already noted some pitfalls in seeking God's power wrongly. However, we don't need to fear if we seek with

---

[177] John 15:26 "When the Helper comes, whom I whom I will send to you from the Father, that is the Spirit of truth who proceeds from the Father, He will testify about Me."

2 Timothy 3:16 "All Scripture is inspired by God and profitable for teaching, for reproof, for correction, for training in righteousness."

See also 2 Peter 1:20-21; John 16:13; 1 Corinthians 12:3

[178] Being overly subjective means elevating your feelings and inner impressions above anything objective outside yourself. It leads inevitably to an illusory and self-centered view of things, to delusion and to divisions among people.

right motives while being submitted to the Bible and the legitimate spiritual authorities God has placed in our lives.

Being Adventurous in the Spirit

God wants us to confidently ask for the Holy Spirit. Jesus made the following promise:

> *Now suppose one of you fathers is asked by his son for a fish; he will not give him a snake instead of a fish, will he? Or if he is asked for an egg, he will not give him a scorpion, will he? If you then, being evil, know how to give good gifts to your children, how much more will your heavenly Father give the Holy Spirit to those who ask Him?* - *Luke 11:11-13*

As you may know, snakes, serpents, and scorpions are symbols of Satan, his demons, and those who follow him.[179] Jesus is saying He wants us to ask for the Holy Spirit and His enablement without fear of the enemy. We should do so confident of God's desire to give us these things.

God wants us to grow in our fruitfulness through the anointing of the Holy Spirit. Rather than be timid, He wants us to take risks in following His Spirit. Now, to take risks doesn't mean that we go beyond the counsel and boundaries of Scripture into dangerous and deceptive, New Age, mystical practices. Rather, it means that we obey what we believe are the promptings of the Holy Spirit. His promptings seldom come with flashing lights and a voice from heaven saying, "Now hear this, this is the Holy Spirit." Rather, they are usually very gentle. We think, "I feel that the Holy Spirit wants me to pray for that person

---

[179] Luke 10:19; Revelation 12:9; Matthew 23:33

behind me in line at the grocery store, but how can I be sure?" Well, the only way to be sure is to obey what you believe the Holy Spirit wants you to do. In this way, we grow in our ability to follow His leading and use His gifts.

Following the Holy Spirit feels "risky" because we do it "by faith, not by sight."[180] It wouldn't take much faith to read a note that was dropped down to us from heaven, but it does take faith to step out in obedience when we aren't sure how our words or actions will be received—especially when we are not 100% certain our leading is from God. But if we aren't willing to step out, then the wonderful works of the Holy Spirit won't be accomplished.

Humility is an Important Key

It helps if you act in a spirit of humility while following what you believe to be the Holy Spirit's leading. You can say, "I can't get away from the feeling that God wants me to pray for you. Is there something troubling you that you would like me to pray for?" Usually, you will find that you were in fact hearing from God, but even if they decline, you did the right thing because you were seeking to be obedient. In the same way, if you are praying for someone and you get a picture in your mind or you think you have a word of prophecy for them, you can say, "I think the Lord is showing me something about your situation. Let me know if this makes sense to you."

If you approach the person in humility, you reduce your fear of obeying the Holy Spirit's promptings and therefore increase your ability to be used by God. Boastful self-assuredness is not necessary. In fact, it is a detriment. The

---

[180] 2 Corinthians 5:7

Bible says, *"God is opposed to the proud, but gives grace [i.e. help and divine empowerment] to the humble."*[181] This means that a person's anointing and giftedness is not increased by self-promotion, boastful claims, and showboating. That may attract followers, but it does not increase the anointing. Humility is what makes us more powerful in God's hands. Jesus said, *"Learn from Me, for I am gentle and humble in heart."*[182]

Having the right attitude is important. Being attuned to the Holy Spirit depends upon developing true humility rather than seeking for personal fulfilment. It requires embracing the work of the cross in our lives rather than celebrating self-esteem. If you want to be a true spiritual leader, you must be willing to challenge the accepted ways and values of an ungodly world, for Christ's sake, rather than checking all the politically correct boxes to gain acceptance and popularity.

The "Suddenness" of God

While we rejoice in the fact that God uses us to bring salvation, healing, and deliverance to the lost and to extend His kingdom, we should, at the same time, always pray for revival. **God has always used such extraordinary times to revive His great work and bend the course of history.** America needs the Church to be salt and light,[183] but it also needs the Lord to *"rend the heavens and come down."*[184]

---

181 James 4:6
182 Matthew 11:29
183 Matthew 5:13-14
184 Isaiah 64:1

The prescription for a degenerating society and a weakened Church is revival. Rather than becoming demoralized by the condition of society around us, we should be inspired to call out to God for revival. Most great revivals and awakenings have been sent when they are most needed, when conditions look bleak and hopeless. Let's consider the Great Revival that began at Pentecost, recorded in Acts 2, as our example.

- It came out of great **defeat:** The nation of Israel had rejected and crucified their Messiah.
- It came out of great **failure:** All the disciples had fled and abandoned Jesus. Peter denied Him.
- It came out of great **distress**: The few followers of Jesus that were left were hiding.

What did they do? They gathered for impassioned prayer.[185] And God answered, not so much because of the passion of their prayers but because God's timing had come. Pentecost was the feast celebrating the annual harvest. This was a foreshadowing of God's great harvest into the Church.

When the day of Pentecost had come, they were all together in one place. And suddenly there came from heaven a noise like a violent rushing wind, and it filled the whole house where they were sitting. And there appeared to them tongues as of fire distributing themselves, and they rested on each one of them. - Acts 2:1-3, emphasis added

---

[185] Acts 1:14

Note that in the midst of very discouraging times, God rent the heavens and "suddenly" answered the prayers of His people and brought revival. It was not just a response to the apostles' prayer but was in response to years of prayer by God's people. God always hears our prayers for revival. They become like pent-up water behind a dam, and then in God's perfect timing, the dam "suddenly" breaks and revival bursts forth like a mighty, rushing flood. If we had time, we could trace this principle through all of the great revivals and awakenings that have ever come.

Many of us have prayed for many years, even decades, for the next mighty outpouring of God. God has heard every prayer. None of them have fallen on deaf ears or been said in vain. We must continue to pray in faith until God "suddenly" answers from heaven in great power. We must not become despondent or discouraged by what we see around us. Our God is faithful.

We must not think that revival is something we can hype up. Rather, they are extraordinary times sent from heaven.

Jonathan Edwards wrote of the First Great Awakening:

"God, in so remarkable a manner took the work into His own hands, there was as much done in a day or two, as at ordinary times...with such a blessing as we commonly have, is done in a year."[186]

Likewise, Frank Bartleman wrote of the great Pentecostal Revival:

---

[186] Edwards, Jonathan. A Faithful Narrative of The Surprising Work of God. Baker Books, reprinted 1979, page 27

"I used to often declare during 1905, that I would rather live six months at that time than fifty years of ordinary time. It was a day of the beginning of great things" [187]

All of the revivalists of the past wrote and spoke of the unusualness of these times. Writing years later, they looked back in awe of the great work of God. Although they were the leaders of those revivals, they realized that they could not reproduce those same conditions again.

Sometimes ministers and groups try to hype up meetings as "revivals." A true revival needs no hype or marketing. I know of many churches that have been hyped or "revived" to death, or at least greatly diminished. Now what kind of a revival leaves people exhausted and disillusioned, with their churches reduced and in financial problems? Such hyped up "revivals" are just largely fruitless distractions. True revivals bring about just the opposite.

If we want to see true revivals that bring life and great, lasting fruit, we must realize God's purposes in sending revival. His purposes are to bring His people to repentance and holiness so that they can experience God's presence and power and to bring in a great harvest of the lost.

A revival isn't an event you attend but a move of God that you become a part of. There is a cost to being part of revival. A revival isn't sent so that I can have great, emotional experiences but so that God's kingdom will advance!

---

[187] Bartleman, Frank. Azusa Street. Logos Books. 1980. Page 21

The Road Ahead

As our study draws to a close, we look forward with faith and expectation. The future of the Church is bright! God's kingdom will continue to advance. God wants to empower each of His children as they employ their gifts because He wants to see lives saved and transformed. He wants to do His works through you and me and see His kingdom extended. God has an adventure ahead for all of us.

And true to His promises, God will again, at His chosen moments, rend the heavens and come down, bringing those extraordinary times of special visitation and revival. In those times, the Church will see His stunning works and witness a wonderful advance of His kingdom. The future of His Church is always bright. Truly, the best is yet to come.

If you have benefited from reading this book, please take a moment to leave a review on amazon.com. If you are interested in reading more from Pastor Mark Hoffman or his brother and co-pastor David, visit:

www.foothillschurch.org/media/bookstore

Made in the USA
Columbia, SC
04 January 2020